Trading Mindset Unlocked

10 Steps To Overcome Fear and Trade With Confidence

RIMANTAS PETRAUSKAS

Trading Mindset Unlocked
10 Steps To Overcome Fear And Trade With Confidence
First Edition

ISBN: 978-609-08-0884-9

Table of Contents

INTRODUCTION

The Real War Isn't With the Market. It's With the Version of You That Panics Under Pressure.

If you're tired of being "almost funded," you're finally holding the manual to fix it.

You don't need another strategy. You don't need another indicator. You don't need another "Top 5 Mistakes Traders Make" YouTube video.

You need one thing: **An identity upgrade.**

Because no matter how good your strategy is... If your identity still belongs to the version of you who needs to be right, chases losses, and folds under pressure, your account won't survive.

And yeah, I know that hits a little hard. It's supposed to.

Look—I've been where you are. Sitting there after another Phase 2 blow-up, refreshing Discord, thinking, "I KNOW this setup works... so why don't I?"

It's not your knowledge. It's not your charts. It's not "bad luck."

It's you.

(And that's good news. Because if you're the problem... you're also the solution.)

This book isn't going to drown you in pep talks. It isn't going to sprinkle some "believe in yourself" fairy dust on your trading plan. It's going to hand you a crowbar and say: **Let's pry the old wiring out and rebuild you properly.**

Here's just a glimpse of what you're about to unlock inside these pages:

The Hidden Identity Leaks Sabotaging Your Trading

- Why your old self keeps hijacking your discipline when the pressure hits.
- How to spot "panic scripts" before they trigger account-killing decisions.

Battle-Tested Rituals That Rewire Your Emotional Reflexes

- The "Cold Click Ritual" that turns impulse trades into sniper entries.
- The "60-Second Stall" that saves you from chasing revenge trades.
- The "Funded Five Simulation" — a 5-day protocol that forges iron discipline under fire.

The Real Science Behind Trading Emotions (Not Just Pop Psychology)

- Why cortisol and adrenaline aren't just feelings — they're sabotage signals.

- How to hack your nervous system back into sniper mode during losses.

How to Stay Funded (When 80% of Traders Lose It All)

- The "Post-Funding Identity Collapse" nobody talks about.
- Why passing a challenge is the audition — but staying funded is the career.

The Iron Mind Protocol

- Not just motivation.
- Not just mindset.
- A full operating system reboot that makes emotional mistakes almost impossible.

Now listen —

If you're still reading, it's because you feel it.

That tension. That frustration. That deep-down "I know I'm close, but something keeps pulling me back" feeling.

I know it too. I lived there for years.

Trading isn't just charts and setups. It's identity warfare.

Every session, you're not fighting the market. You're fighting the undisciplined version of you that wants to:

- Chase a half-baked setup because it "feels right."
- Double size after a loss to "make it back."
- Cut a winner early because you "can't stand the pullback."

That version of you isn't evil. It's just **untrained.**

This book is your boot camp. Your field manual. Your cold, clear mirror.

Who Am I To Tell You This?

My name is **Rimantas Petrauskas**, and I've been walking this road since 2009.

Not as a guru. Not as some fast-talking marketer with a Lambo and a dream. But as a guy who hit rock bottom and built his way back with nothing but a decision.

In 2009, I was overweight, broke, stuck in a toxic relationship, and questioning whether life was supposed to feel that heavy.

So I made a choice. I lost 30 kg. I got out of debt. I walked away from the things holding me down. And I started a business from scratch to help Forex traders like me stop struggling in the dark.

Since then, I've built tools like **Local Trade Copier** and **FxMagnetic** that have helped thousands of traders in over 100 countries.

I've written two books, taught traders worldwide, and developed a system that helps people build strategies and test them — not on hope, but on data.

But none of that matters if you don't know this:

I'm not here because everything always worked out. I'm here because it didn't. Because I've blown it. Failed. Wanted to quit.

And I didn't.

I kept going. I adapted. I rebuilt. I turned my pain into process.

The tools I've built aren't magic. They're systems. Reliable, scalable, and backed by mental resilience I earned mile by mile — including trail running races as long as 69 kilometers.

That's what I want to give you. Not fluff. Not hype. Just the real stuff that works, if you do.

So if you're tired of guessing, tired of the rollercoaster, tired of being "almost funded"... You're in the right place.

Let's unlock the version of you who doesn't flinch under pressure. Let's train the identity that can hold a funded account and thrive.

Let's win this thing — from the inside out.

Why This Book Is Different

Most trading books either:

- Dump a bunch of strategies on you without addressing execution,
- Or give you "mindset advice" that's basically "Think positive thoughts, bro."

Neither works.

You don't need more strategies. You don't need another vision board. You need a **battle plan**. You need **rituals**. You need a **system to rebuild the you** who shows up at the charts.

That's what this book gives you. Step-by-step. Systematically. Relentlessly.

Because here's the brutal truth:

You don't rise to the level of your dreams. You fall to the level of your identity.

And right now, your identity — not your strategy — is deciding whether you win or lose.

Here's What Happens Next

In the next few chapters, we're going to:

- Shatter the "market is against me" myth once and for all.
- Map out the invisible traps that sabotage 9 out of 10 traders.
- Train you to execute like a professional, even under pressure.
- Rebuild your internal operating system until discipline is automatic.

You're going to hurt a little. You're going to confront some ugly truths. You're going to leave parts of your old trading self behind.

Good.

Because when we're done? You're not just going to trade better. You're going to **be** better.

Ready to stop playing small? Ready to stop "almost" making it? Ready to finally **become the trader** you know you're meant to be?

Turn the page.

Your evolution starts now.

CHAPTER 1

The Mirror Isn't Lying – Why the Market Exposes You

The market reflects your mindset, not your methods.

Reality Check Before We Begin

Let's not sugarcoat it: trading is one of the hardest careers in the world.

It's not hard because of math. It's not hard because of indicators or news events. It's hard because it forces you to confront yourself every single day. It holds up a mirror to your psychology, your discipline, your emotions, and your identity—on loop.

We're not saying this to demotivate you. We're saying it because the first rule of any battle is to know what you're up against. Sun Tzu said, "If you know the enemy and know yourself, you need not fear the result of a hundred battles."

But here's the twist: in trading, the market is not the enemy. The enemy is within. The real opponent is the reactive, ego-driven version of you that shows up under pressure. And if you want to win this battle, you've got to study yourself like the market studies you.

This chapter is the beginning of that study.

And like all good beginnings, this one starts with acceptance. Acceptance that you are not just learning a skill—you are reshaping your identity. You are not entering a game. You are stepping onto a battlefield. Not to fight the market, but to fight for your evolution.

Trading reveals your weaknesses in real time. Unlike most jobs, there is no manager, no structure, no external accountability. Your only guide is the version of you that shows up each day—and if that version isn't trained, disciplined, and emotionally stable, the market will exploit every crack. This isn't a career for dabblers. It's a high-stakes mirror reflecting the truest parts of you. And the sooner you face that reflection, the sooner you start gaining real control.

It's not about having more knowledge—it's about having fewer leaks. Fewer moments where your old identity hijacks your trades. Fewer emotional shortcuts. Fewer self-sabotaging patterns that play out under pressure. Trading isn't just a performance of skill. It's a practice of psychological endurance.

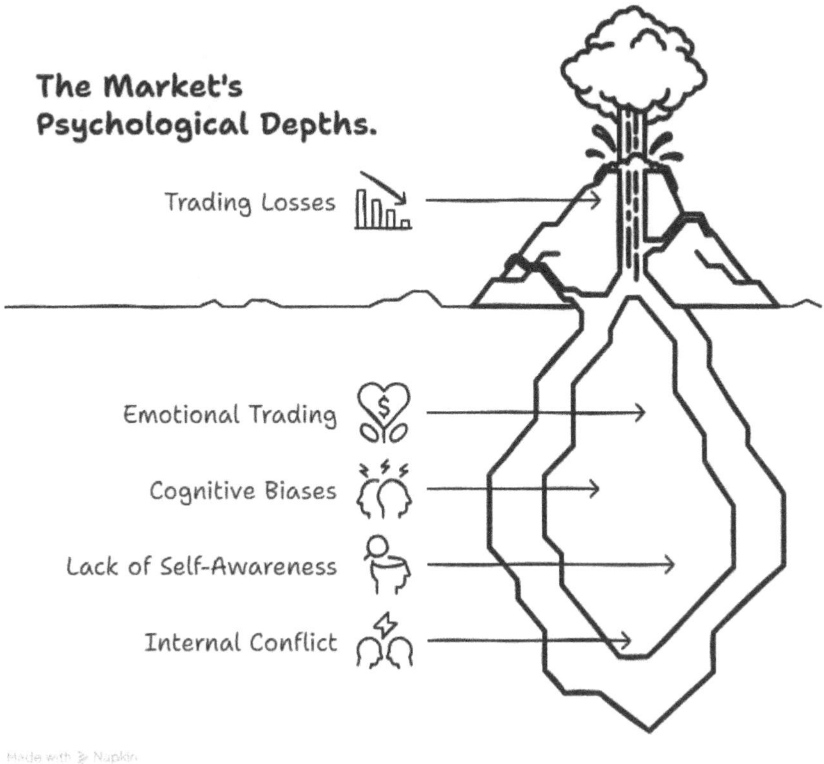

The Market as a Psychological Opponent

Let's get something straight right now: the market is not your friend. It's not your mentor. It doesn't care how badly you want it, how many YouTube videos you've watched, or how many Phase 1s you've passed. The market is a psychological opponent—a mirror with no filter. It doesn't just test your strategy; it exposes your identity.

Every time you open a chart, you're not trading against candlesticks. You're trading against institutions armed with data scientists, AI, and psychological models that know exactly when you're going to flinch. It's not a conspiracy theory. It's math. It's behavioral economics. It's *you* being predictable under pressure.

Think of the market like a military sniper who doesn't just wait for movement—they study your breathing. They know when you'll hesitate, chase, or bail. They don't need to beat you with firepower. They just need to let you beat yourself.

Take the "Dumb Money Effect"—an academic term, not a meme. Retail traders, according to Coval & Shumway (2005), consistently buy at tops and sell at bottoms. Why? Because emotion—not logic—guides most decisions. Institutions know this. They use volume, speed, and fake breakouts to trigger your FOMO, your fear, your need to be right. And you walk into it like a trap.

This isn't about being dumb. It's about being *emotional*. And the market is engineered to make you emotional.

The more aware you become of your own cognitive loops, the less you'll become bait. And that awareness? It starts with accepting that the market is not out to get you—it's out to *expose* you.

The most dangerous trader in the world isn't the one with the best setup. It's the one with nothing left to prove. The one who has made peace with discomfort. The one who knows the enemy isn't on the other side of the chart—it's the voice in their own head that whispers "just this once."

In a way, the market is more honest than most people you'll meet. It doesn't lie to you. It doesn't flatter you. It simply reflects who you are at that moment. And that reflection? That's your edge—or your downfall.

The more skilled you become, the more subtle the challenges. At first, the battle is external—learning structure, finding setups, executing with consistency. But soon, the battle becomes internal. Can you remain still during chaos? Can you follow your rules after five losses in a row? Can you sit out when every cell in your body is screaming, "Enter now!" This is when trading stops being a skillset and starts being a mirror.

The Casino with Better Suits

Picture this: a casino floor. But instead of roulette wheels and slot machines, there are candlestick charts and news headlines. Everyone thinks they have an edge. Everyone thinks they're the exception. But just like a casino, the house always wins—unless you learn the game *behind* the game.

Institutions are the house. Retail traders are the tourists. And the chart is just the flashy interface.

Ever taken a trade that looked perfect on paper—clean setup, all confirmations—and it still failed? That's not bad luck. That's manipulation. Institutions create fake breakouts knowing exactly where most stop-losses are sitting. They design traps that prey on your emotional predictability.

A 2023 report from FTMO showed that over 80% of traders who pass Phase 1 fail within weeks of getting funded. The setups don't change. *The psychology does.*

The biggest myth in trading? That success comes from knowing more. In reality, it comes from *reacting less.*

The market isn't a mystery. It's a psychological game dressed up in data. And every time you act out of urgency or fear, you're feeding the house.

Every single time you click out of a trade early to "secure profits," or chase a move that already ran, or size up because you want to make back what you lost yesterday—you are the house's favorite player. Because you think you're playing the game, but you are the game.

To beat the casino, you don't just need discipline—you need detachment. The kind of detachment that makes you walk away from a perfect-looking setup because it's not aligned with your rules. The kind of discipline that lets you take a loss with zero emotional charge, because you know it was a clean execution.

Professional traders don't win because they avoid pain. They win because they embrace it on purpose, and learn how to bleed without flinching.

The casino metaphor might sound harsh, but it's a perfect mirror of reality. You need to trade like the house. Patient. Disciplined. Unmoved by emotion. Focused only on edge and repetition. That's how you build consistency.

If trading is a casino, then your job is to be the one running the table—not throwing chips hoping for luck. It's about probability, edge, and emotional stamina. And like the best casinos in the world, you need systems, structure, and the ability to enforce rules no matter how exciting the game gets. Otherwise, the game will play you.

The Identity Leak

Let's go deeper: Your trading account is not a portfolio—it's a mirror. It reflects your habits, your discipline, and your self-control.

Every undisciplined trade you take isn't a strategy problem—it's an identity leak. It's the *"almost"* version of you taking the wheel again.

The one who says, "Just this once," or "I'll size down next time." That version of you isn't random. It's rehearsed.

Your rituals reveal your results. If you open your charts with no clear plan, scroll social media between trades, or adjust stops mid-trade out of fear—you're not trading the strategy. You're trading *you*.

And here's the brutal truth: The market doesn't care about your intentions. It only responds to your execution.

Your ego wants to win. Your identity wants to survive. Only one of them has the patience to trade well.

Discipline is not motivation. It's identity. If you identify as someone who follows rules under pressure, you trade like it. If you don't, no setup in the world will save you.

Let's be real: You can have the cleanest strategy in the world. You can pass five challenges back to back. But if your identity is still wired for validation, revenge, or self-sabotage, the account won't survive. Because accounts don't blow up from red candles—they blow up from weak identity scripts.

If you want to upgrade your trading, don't start with more screen time. Start with the story you're telling yourself. Rewrite it. Edit ruthlessly. Become the version of you who already trades like a pro—before the market forces you to become him the hard way.

And that begins with your habits. Your rituals. The invisible moments where no one's watching. That's where identity is either reinforced—or broken.

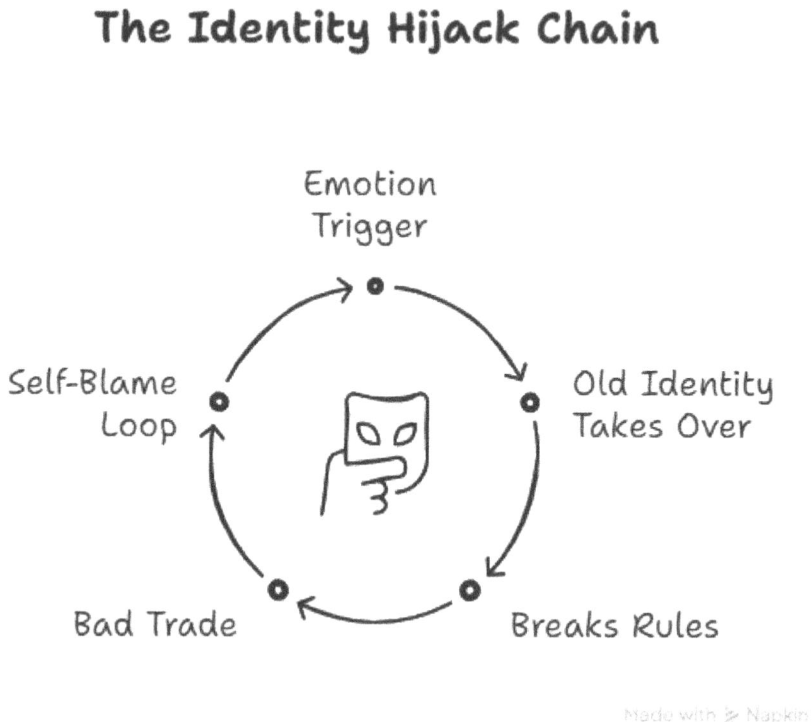

Mini-Missions (Behavioral Drills)

These aren't suggestions. They're psychological armor. Pick one each week. Repeat until it's instinct.

1. The Blindfold Week

Trade with all indicators turned off. Pure price action. Forces emotional awareness and intuition.

I once did this myself. No indicators. Just candlesticks and raw price. That week, I learned more than I had in months. I began to understand pinbars, three white soldiers, three black crows—candlestick patterns that reveal the emotional DNA of the market. I saw how they repeat.

But I also saw how the market *manipulates* these patterns. It was both enlightening and frustrating. But more than anything, it was training—not just for my eyes, but for my mind. I started to see price as behavior, not just structure.

You'll be shocked at how much cleaner the market looks when you remove the noise. And you'll also see how much of your trading was just reacting to colors and indicators, not actual logic. This week will humble you—and that's the point.

It's like learning to box with a blindfold on. You stop relying on your eyes and start tuning into rhythm, pressure, and flow. You start feeling what the market wants—not in a mystical way, but in a way that teaches you to sense behavior before you react to it. This week will teach you emotional accuracy. That's a superpower.

2. The 60-Second Stall

Before every entry or exit, pause for 60 seconds. Break the reflex loop. Decide, don't react.

This used to be my biggest weakness. I would see my setup forming, price moving fast, and I'd pounce. Click. I'm in. Seconds later, price would reverse, take me out at my stop, and then continue in my direction—without me. It felt like someone was on the other side, watching, laughing. But that's not paranoia. That's *market structure.* That's how manipulation works.

Eventually, I broke free from it by automating my entries and removing my impulse from the equation. But before automation, this one-second impulse cost me months of progress. That's why the 60-second stall matters. Even 30 seconds can save you from a psychological landmine.

That delay is where discipline lives. It's where clarity forms. In that silence, you get to ask: is this trade aligned with my rules—or my emotions?

The habit of waiting changes how your brain works. It rewires your relationship with urgency. It gives your rational mind time to overrule your emotional reflex. That tiny pause? It's a wedge between chaos and control. Make it sacred.

3. The Cold Click Ritual

Take a cold shower, then place your first trade. Link discomfort to clarity. Train calm under pressure.

I used to *hate* the cold. I couldn't even take mildly chilly showers. But one winter, I decided to face it head-on. I started swimming in ice-cold water with a group that met weekly. We'd cut a hole in the ice and plunge in—sometimes when it was -20°C. I did it for weeks. Then for multiple winters. It didn't just kill my fear of cold water. It rewired my identity. I became someone who could choose discomfort—on purpose.

As traders, that's everything. We need to choose discomfort over impulse. Cold showers aren't just physical. They are mindset reps. I'm not telling you to jump into frozen lakes, but if you want to build grit? Get cold. Get uncomfortable. Then get calm.

There's a quiet power that comes from doing hard things with no audience. Cold water becomes a metaphor. If you can face that without flinching, the markets start to feel a little less threatening. Because you've trained your nervous system to stay steady under pressure. And trading is pressure, distilled.

4. Emotional Self-Audit

Rate yourself post-trade on: Patience, Confidence, Discipline (1–10). Track patterns, not just PnL.

I do this myself. I'm not a guru. I'm a trader in progress—just like you. Some weeks, I rate myself an 8. I feel sharp. Focused. Other weeks? A 4. Impulsive. Distracted. That's when I know it's time to pause. Time for a trading break. Not forever. Just long enough to recalibrate.

Because the market will always be there. But your mindset? That needs protection. It needs recovery. This audit keeps me honest. Keeps me evolving.

This exercise will teach you that trading isn't about being perfect—it's about staying aware. Awareness is your edge. And the moment you stop reflecting, you start repeating.

Your account is a journal. But it only makes sense if you treat it like data. The numbers are feedback, but the emotions underneath? That's the real signal. The Emotional Self-Audit gives you the truth your PnL can't show.

5. The Funded Five Simulation

For five days, execute every trade *as if* you're already managing a six-figure account. No emotion, no deviation. Journal everything.

If you can do this, even for one day, you'll feel the shift. You'll start to trade from identity, not desperation. This is the challenge that breaks the old you.

Here's a secret: The market doesn't give you a funded account so you can become a pro. It gives you capital to *reveal* who you already are. The Funded Five is your audition. You're not waiting to be chosen. You're proving you already belong.

When you raise your standards, the market responds. Not because it's magical, but because your execution becomes so consistent that randomness can't shake you. The Funded Five isn't just a drill. It's a transformation protocol.

Let me tell you a story…

We were on a family vacation in the French Riviera. The kids had fallen in love with *Mr. Bean's Holiday*, so we traced parts of his silly journey—starting in Paris, having breakfast at Le Train Bleu in Gare de Lyon, then heading to Cannes by train. On the last day of the trip, we were staying in Nice. The kids wanted a lazy day at the hotel pool. I smiled and said, "Sure"—but inside, I knew I needed a personal mission.

At dawn, while everyone slept, I laced up my shoes and slipped out the door. My target? Monaco. About 20 km along the coast. The sun was just rising, and I ran past pastel-colored villages, cliffs dropping into turquoise water, ancient stone walls, and winding streets. When I hit Monaco, I felt good. Too good to stop.

So I kept going.

I reached Menton, a quiet town near the Italian border, I always wanted to visit this small town because my friend Alex had once lived there and always was telling me how nice it is. He was right, it is a very nice town.

Then, I looked at the map and saw Ventimiglia, a town in Italy just across the border. I smiled—this could be epic. France, Monaco, Italy. One run. Fifty kilometers.

I pushed through tired legs, sore feet, and the weight of solitude. Finally, I hit the town, took a deep breath, snapped a photo, and hopped a train back.

That run wasn't for glory. It was a lesson. A reminder that we can create adventure. That mental toughness can be disguised as curiosity. And that pushing boundaries doesn't require an audience—just the willingness to go a bit further than yesterday.

These are the moments that build your mindset.

I didn't do this for medals. I did it because I crave the unusual. The blend of curiosity and challenge becomes a mindset rep: running through discomfort *because your spirit says, "Let's go."* These mini-missions aren't about grand gestures—they're about proving to your brain that you *won't quit when it's hard*. They're about finding creativity, excitement, and growth in your everyday life.... and maybe getting an epic Strava post to show the grandchildren someday.

The Endurance Standard

> "The market doesn't test your strategy. It tests your emotional control. And every trade you take is either proof of discipline—or evidence that your identity still needs work."

Let's frame this with a story most people miss.

Imagine a prop firm wasn't hiring traders—but distance runners. Now imagine they announced the standard: to qualify, you need to run **1**

mile in 3 minutes and 43.13 seconds. That's the world record, set by Hicham El Guerrouj. No one else on earth has ever hit that time. Even Hicham himself might not be able to repeat it today.

So the firm lowers the bar—run a mile in under **8 minutes**. That's much more achievable, but still out of reach for most casual runners. And if you show up huffing after a 12-minute jog, it's clear you're not ready for funding. The truth is, you can't fake elite fitness. And you can't fake elite trading discipline either.

Now here's where most traders miss the metaphor: running **one** mile fast is like **passing a prop firm challenge**. It's just Stage One. But what happens next? What happens when the real journey begins and you're asked to **sustain** that pace—not for one mile, but for dozens? For months? For years?

That's what prop firms are really testing: **endurance**, not just performance.

And this is where I bring in a bit of my own story.

I'm not a fast runner. Never have been. But I've run long. **Really long.** My personal best is **69 kilometers in a single go**. I've trained my mind not to give up after 10km, not after 30km, and definitely not after 50km. When your legs scream, your joints ache, and your mind says "stop"—something deeper takes over. That's mindset. That's endurance.

And my biggest test? A nine-day run across Lithuania: **500 kilometers**, averaging 40–69km per day. Day after day. Morning to night. Pain, blisters, rain, fatigue—and I kept running. Not because I'm superhuman, but because I built a mindset that didn't depend on motivation. I trained myself to keep going when everything else wanted to quit.

That's the kind of trader prop firms are looking for.
Not the one who can hit a lucky streak. Not the one who nails a challenge after a good week. They want the one who can keep going. Through slumps. Through doubt. Through days when the market humbles you. They want the trader who has built the mental strength to stay sharp for months—and then sharpen again.

The challenge phase is the sprint. But the funded journey is the marathon. And only those who train for both will thrive.

This book isn't about teaching you how to pass a challenge. It's about building the **trader who can last**. The kind of person who doesn't just survive tough conditions—but gets stronger in them.

This chapter was your starting line.

From here on, we train endurance. Mindset. Identity. Discipline.

Welcome to the run of your life.

10 Underground Hacks for Psychological Mastery in Trading

These tactics weren't invented by me—they were collected. I've found them in trading books, deep-dive tutorials, YouTube videos, and the occasional private group or paid course. Some are well-hidden, others are just underused—but together, they form a playbook of practical, powerful ways to upgrade how you trade.

1. "Alt Account Mentality" Hack

Use a second account with deliberately *smaller* capital just to train psychology.
Institutional traders sometimes simulate *impossible risk parameters* to build detachment. The pressure's off because the stakes are fake—but the decisions are real. You'll notice impulsive habits much faster here.

> 💡 *Secret: Funded account evaluators use similar psych traps in their challenges to test your reactions under fake stress.*

2. Replay Mode Ritual *(Gray Hat Insight)*

Use TradingView's *Bar Replay* or NinjaTrader's Market Replay to **re-watch your own trades in 2x speed with audio recording of your thoughts.**
You're basically building a *game tape* for your brain. Pro traders do this and narrate their emotions out loud. Then rewatch it as if coaching a student. Brutally effective for catching identity leaks.

3. Subvocal Trigger Pattern

Track *invisible micro-gestures* (like biting your lip, tapping a pen) that occur right before you make emotional trades.

This is **micro-kinesthetic awareness training**—a technique adapted from CIA-level behavioral analysis. Once you can catch the *trigger*, you can interrupt the loop *before* the decision.

4. Risk Tag Journal System

Every trade must be tagged with a *"Risk Identity Tag"* before execution:

- Revenge Risk

- Ego Risk
- Desperation Risk
- Clean System

Force yourself to assign one label. This creates an internal interrupt and forces identity awareness into the decision moment.

> *Optional twist: Post the tag in a private trading group before executing.*

5. Dead Account Drill

Create a mock account and intentionally **blow it up within 5 trades—*on purpose*.**

But: You must *journal every emotional decision*. This reverse drill gives *permission to fail fast* and see exactly how sabotage scripts activate under no constraint. Wildly clarifying.

6. The "Anti-Entry" Watchlist

Keep a separate watchlist of trades you *wanted* to enter impulsively but **chose not to.**

Review it weekly. This shows you the *power of restraint* in real numbers. Often, these trades would've been losers—which builds massive subconscious trust in your new identity.

7. Three-Strikes Micro Discipline Contract

Write a 3-strike rule for a single behavior leak (e.g., moving stop-loss, revenge trade).

If you violate it 3x in one week, you must take 3 full days off from live trading. This mimics *institutional probation protocols* and conditions high-level accountability fast.

8. Synthetic Anxiety Trigger

Before your trading session, watch **your own worst loss replay**, or revisit a painful trading memory.

Why? To intentionally **trigger pre-session anxiety** in a *controlled setting*. Then execute through it. You're training emotional regulation under synthetic market stress.

> ⚠ *Gray Hat: Can be emotionally intense. Only use this drill once every few weeks.*

9. Opposite-Hand Execution

Trade one session using only your **non-dominant hand** to click entries/exits.

This disrupts unconscious behavior patterns and forces present-moment focus. Traders report a sudden decrease in overtrading and reactive clicks.

10. Trade Like You're Being Watched (Surveillance Effect)

Set up a screen recorder or webcam—not for reviewing PnL, but just to **simulate being observed.**

Known as the *Hawthorne Effect,* this trick from performance psychology makes you less likely to deviate from plan because your brain believes it's being judged.

Final Thought

These aren't standard tips—they're **psychological upgrades disguised as drills.** You're not just improving your edge... you're eliminating the behaviors that destroy it. Use responsibly, test in simulation first, and remember:

> **You don't rise to the level of your plan. You fall to the level of your identity.**

In the next chapter, we're going to pull back the curtain on one of the most dangerous mindset traps in trading. It's the emotional loop that turns one mistake into five. That turns a small loss into a blown account.

We call it **The B.R.E.A.K. Loop.**

It's the unconscious pattern that keeps even talented traders stuck in frustration, sabotage, and regret. But once you see the loop? You can break it. You can interrupt the cycle and start creating new outcomes.

So, take a breath. You've just finished the first workout. Now it's time to sharpen your sword.

Let's go deeper. Let's break the loop.

CHAPTER 2

The B.R.E.A.K. Loop – How Traders Fall Into Destructive Mindset Cycles

The loop that breaks your consistency before the market ever does.

The Pattern You Don't See—But Always Feel

You didn't lose because of the strategy. You didn't blow the account because of one bad trade. The downfall didn't happen in your TradingView. It happened in your mind—long before you clicked the button.

If you're like most traders, your worst trades don't come from lack of knowledge. They come from emotional overdrive. From identity confusion. From falling into a loop that feels like progress but is actually just well-dressed sabotage.

We call it the **B.R.E.A.K. Loop**.

This isn't just a catchy acronym. It's the invisible spiral that drags traders down. And unless you see it, you'll repeat it. Over and over again. Even after you pass a challenge. Even after you get funded.

Because passing is easy. Sustaining is a whole other game.

Let's break it down.

The B.R.E.A.K. Loop Defined

The B.R.E.A.K. Loop: How Traders Spiral

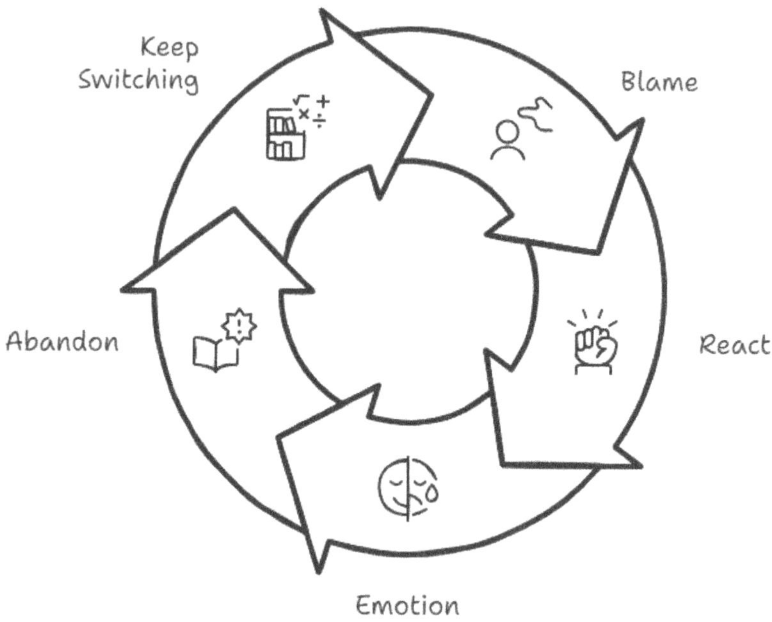

B — Blame

You take a loss. And instead of reflecting inward, you look outward. "The market was manipulated." "The spread jumped." "News came early." Even if you're right, blame is the first brick in a mental wall. Because blame blocks growth. It protects your ego, but imprisons your potential.

R — React

Once you blame, you give away responsibility. That means you're no longer trading with presence. You're reacting. You take the next trade emotionally. You chase. You size up. You deviate. You stop seeing setups clearly because you're too busy proving something—to the market, to your mentor, to yourself.

E — Emotion

Now you're deep in the fog. Your strategy is blurry. Your rules are flexible. Your vision is distorted. You feel frustration, fear, urgency. And you call it intuition—but it's just inflammation. You're no longer trading with logic. You're trading with adrenaline.

A — Abandon

At this stage, the old version of you comes out. You ditch your process. You stop journaling. You stop following your plan. You skip the pre-trade ritual. You say, "I'll fix this later." This is identity regression. You've abandoned the pro inside you and reverted to the gambler, the revenge trader, the hopeful amateur.

K — Keep Switching

Finally, you start looking for the next best thing. "Maybe this strategy isn't it." "Maybe I need indicators." "Maybe I should scalp." "Maybe I'll switch pairs." You become the nomad trader. Always moving, never mastering. You're not evolving—you're escaping.

And just like that, the loop resets. You go back to BLAME.

You never fix the real problem. Because the real problem was never the strategy—it was the loop.

The Strategy Addiction Loop

The B.R.E.A.K. Loop isn't just about mindset. It's also how strategy addiction gets born.

You think you're optimizing. But you're actually running from discomfort.

Let's walk through it:

You find a new strategy. You feel hope. You demo it. It works. You get funded—or close. Then the inevitable happens: the market throws a curveball. A loss streak. A false breakout. Maybe news. Maybe just randomness.

You doubt the system. You tweak it. Then tweak it more. Then you abandon it. Then—you guessed it—you go find another one.

This isn't optimization. It's avoidance.

The belief that "a better strategy will save me" is the biggest lie in retail trading. Because no strategy is immune to drawdown. And drawdown isn't the issue—**your reaction to drawdown is.**

Let's make this plain:

- A new system won't fix your execution problem.
- Changing setups won't erase your overtrading habit.
- More knowledge won't beat emotional chaos.

Execution > Prediction. Always.

The pros don't predict better. They execute cleaner. They lose better. They stick longer. And most importantly—they trust their system enough to see it through the storm.

Until you do the same, you'll keep mistaking hope for progress.

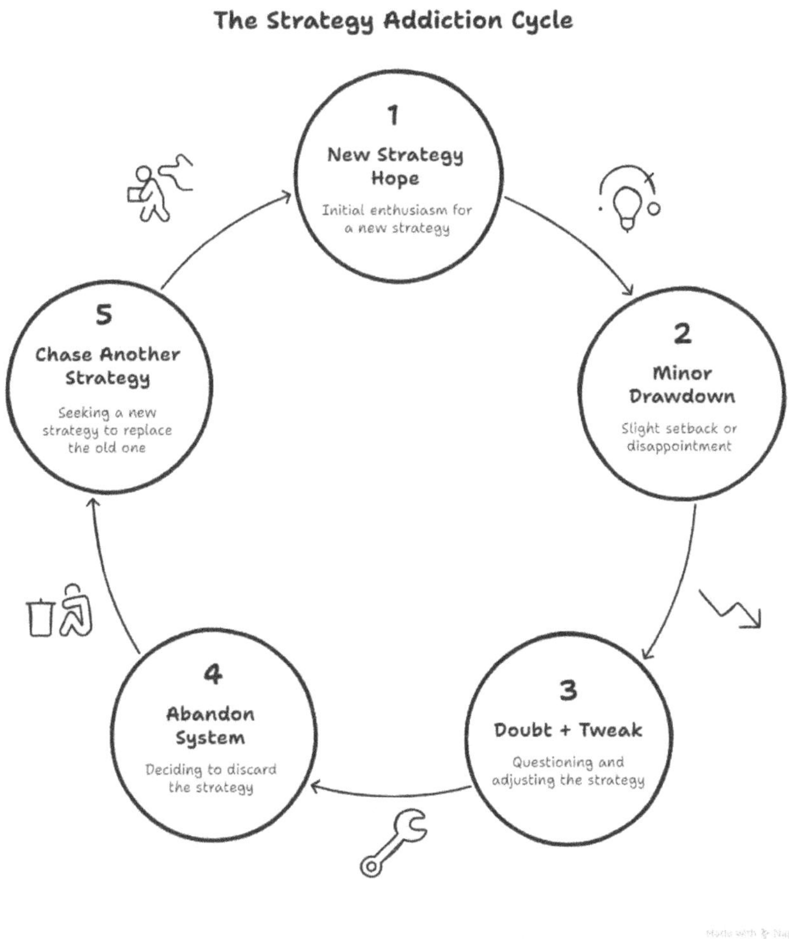

Breaking the Loop

You want to stop the loop? Here's how.

It's not a motivational speech. It's not about affirmations. It's process.

These are five core drills to rewire your brain, rebuild your habits, and restore your control:

1. The 5-Day Rule Commitment

Pick one strategy. One timeframe. One risk model. Commit for five straight trading days—no deviations. You're not trying to win. You're trying to prove you can stay consistent under boredom, losses, and silence.

Good Example:
A trader picks a simple moving average crossover system on the 15-minute chart and sticks with 1% risk per trade. Even after three losses in a row, they log the trades, stay emotionally neutral, and keep executing according to the rules.

Bad Example:
Day two hits a loss, and the trader decides to change pairs and switch from 15-minute to 5-minute to "speed up recovery." By day three, they've added a new indicator and exited the original plan entirely.

2. Strategy Jail

Create a "strategy contract." Lock yourself into a specific system for 30 days. If you want to try something new, fine—write it down, and revisit it after the 30. This prevents impulsive shifts and builds emotional friction around changing plans.

Good Example:
A trader signs their strategy contract and tapes it to the wall. Even when tempted to try scalping during news, they stay within their planned high-probability zone entries on the 1-hour chart.

Bad Example:
On week two, they join a webinar hyping a new Fibonacci tool. They abandon their plan mid-session and convince themselves the switch is "just this once." It turns into their new strategy by the end of the week.

3. Journal Without Judgment

After each session, write what happened—factually. Don't praise. Don't punish. Just document. When you remove judgment, you start seeing patterns clearly. You stop hiding from the truth. And that truth becomes your edge.

Good Example:
Trader journals, "3 trades. 1 win, 2 losses. Followed risk rules. Entered early once, need to recheck trigger criteria." Simple. Clear. No drama.

Bad Example:
Trader writes, "Horrible day! Market is unfair! I suck at this!" or worse—skips journaling altogether when things go badly.

4. Loss Autopsy Drill

Take your last five losing trades and analyze them like a forensic scientist. Was it execution? Emotional entry? Poor structure? News? Self-sabotage? Categorize each one. Now look for the trend. That trend is your real strategy weakness.

Good Example:
After reviewing five losses, the trader sees four of them were from trades taken without waiting for confirmation. They realize impatience is the root issue and adjust their rules accordingly.

Bad Example:
Trader blames "market conditions" for every loss and fails to find any common cause. No change, no insight, and the loop continues.

5. Mental Model Rewiring

Each morning, review your identity statement. Example: "I'm a process-first trader who executes with patience, not emotion." Repeat it. Visualize it. Act it. Make it your baseline. You're not just repeating words—you're reprogramming your brain under pressure.

Good Example:
Before every trading session, the trader says their identity script aloud, takes a few deep breaths, visualizes a clean session, and journals their pre-market thoughts.

Bad Example:
Trader skips the ritual and jumps into the market cold. After a revenge trade, they say, "I'll be more disciplined tomorrow," but take no steps to install that behavior.

None of this is sexy. It's not flashy. But it works. And if you don't build your mental system, no trading system will ever work for you.

Neurological Warfare

You want to trade like a pro? You've got to start by taking care of the machine that makes all your decisions: **your brain.**

I'm not just talking about being "in the right mindset." I'm talking about **how your nervous system, hormones, and brain chemistry are either helping you trade—or sabotaging every setup.**

You can't out-strategy a brain that's under siege.

Let's go deeper. And this time, I want you to actually feel the cost of ignoring these truths—and the power of doing something about them.

Emotional Capital: Your Hidden Bank Account

Every trader knows about financial capital. But emotional capital? That's the one most people only realize when it's already gone.

Here's what emotional capital looks like in real life:

- You hesitate to take your setup.
- You double your risk out of frustration.
- You stare at charts hoping to "see" something.
- You walk away feeling drained—even if you made money.

These aren't discipline issues. These are emotional overdrafts. You've spent too much of your focus, patience, and energy on low-quality decisions—and now you've got nothing left in the tank.

Why this matters: When your emotional capital is empty, your best thinking shuts down. You *will* make mistakes. You *will* repeat old habits. And you won't even realize you're doing it—until your account pays the price.

What to do about it: Set hard boundaries. Trade only during your optimal focus window. Stop when you hit your max number of trades. Journal how you feel—not just what you did.

You manage money. Now manage your **mental budget.**

Cortisol: The Silent Saboteur

Stress is not some vague emotional state—it's a literal chemical process in your brain.

When you take a trade and it instantly goes red, your brain floods with cortisol and adrenaline. Your body reacts like you've been attacked. Fight, flight, or freeze kicks in. Logical thought? Gone. Perspective? Gone.

And guess what? The next decision you make is *almost guaranteed* to be wrong.

Want proof? Think about the last time you revenge traded. Or scaled into a losing trade. Or cut a winner too early because you couldn't handle watching a pullback.

That wasn't a lack of skill. That was a **stress response.**

Why this matters: The more you let stress lead your trades, the more you condition your brain to respond to trading like trauma. Over time, this creates anxiety, hesitation, and even fear of the charts.

What to do about it: Breathe before you enter. Stand up between trades. Shake it off—literally. Even 10 jumping jacks can break the pattern. Use cold water, meditation, or anything that resets your nervous system.

You don't need more willpower. You need **state control**.

Two Brains: One Helps You Win, The Other Helps You Lose

System 1: fast, automatic, emotional.
System 2: slow, logical, rational.

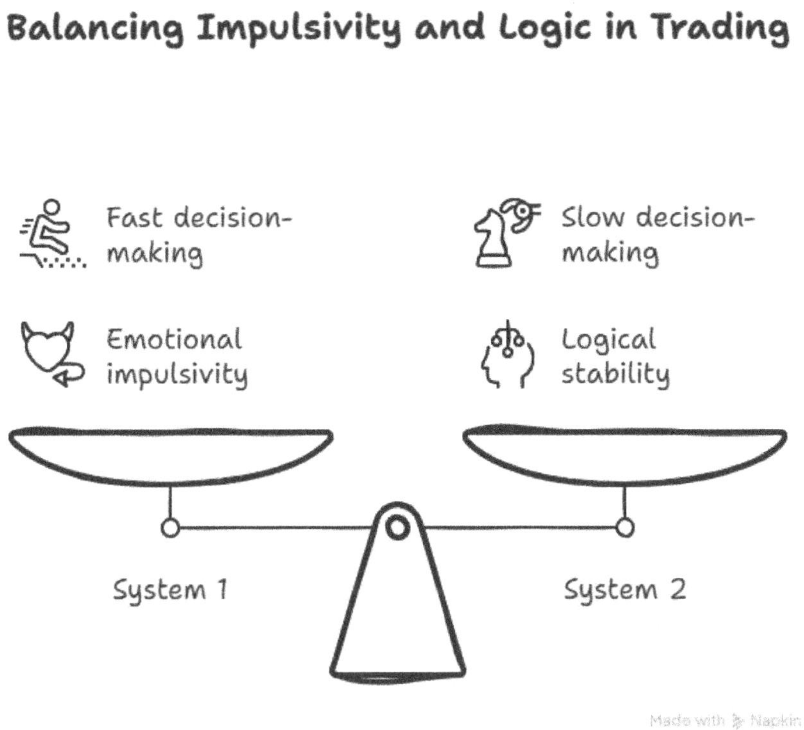

When you're calm, System 2 runs the show. You stick to your plan. You wait for confirmation. You follow your rules.

But under stress, fatigue, or FOMO? System 1 takes over. And that part of your brain doesn't care about your checklist. It just wants *out*—out of discomfort, out of fear, out of the unknown.

Why this matters: Most traders live in System 1 and don't even know it. They make 90% of their decisions from impulse—then try to justify them afterward. That's not trading. That's gambling with nice vocabulary.

What to do about it: Slow down your process. Force yourself to write down your setup before entry. Rate your emotional state. Ask, "Am I thinking fast right now? Or thinking clearly?"

You don't just need a good system. You need to make sure the **right version of you** is the one executing it.

Mental Fatigue: The Invisible Risk Factor

Fatigue doesn't hit you like a bus. It sneaks in.

You start skipping your checklist. You start scanning faster. You lower your standards. You "just want to be in a trade."

Before you know it, your sharp, strategic brain is on autopilot—and you're throwing darts in the dark.

Why this matters: A tired brain is a biased brain. It sees what it wants to see. It convinces itself that "close enough" is good enough. And it forgets the part where you're managing risk with real money.

What to do about it: Timebox your trading. 90 minutes on, 30 minutes off. Schedule rest like you schedule entries. Walk. Eat. Disconnect. Reboot your brain like it's part of your edge—because it is.

Professional traders don't trade more. They trade **sharper**.

Mindfulness: Not Fluff. Function.

Think mindfulness is just for yoga people and monks? Cool—stay impulsive.

Mindfulness is actually a high-performance habit. It's what keeps you from bringing your baggage into the charts. It's what resets you when you're off. It's how you become the version of you that trades clean—even after losses.

Why this matters: Every mistake you've ever made in trading happened in the 2 seconds between emotion and decision. Mindfulness gives you those 2 seconds back.

What to do about it: Build a pre-trade ritual. Light stretching. 60 seconds of deep breathing. Write down your intention. Even a single breath can reset your nervous system—and stop a mistake before it starts.

The market doesn't reward hustle. It rewards presence.

If You Take Nothing Else From This Chapter...

...take this:

You are not a machine. You're a biological, emotional, reactive human being. And if you don't account for that in your process, you'll keep wondering why "perfect setups" keep going wrong.

Trading isn't about seeing more setups. It's about showing up in the right state to **execute** the ones you already know.

Your nervous system is your edge—or your enemy.

Choose wisely.

Takeaway Principle

> "You can't fix emotional chaos with strategic tweaks. You break the loop by building the identity that doesn't enter it in the first place."

Here's the truth you've been avoiding:

It was never the strategy.

It was never the market.

It was never the missed entry, the late news, the fakeout.

It was you—stuck in the loop. Blame, React, Emotion, Abandon, Keep switching. Round and round. Some traders ride that loop for months. Others, for years. And some never get off.

But if you're still reading, that's not going to be you.

You now know the pattern. You see the trap. And most importantly—you have tools to break it.

Drills. Rituals. Identity work. Mental models. The next time you feel the loop pulling you in, pause. Breathe. Audit. Redirect. You don't have to be perfect. You just have to be self-aware.

This chapter was about disruption—interrupting the old cycles that were keeping you in chaos. But Chapter 3? That's about exposure. Because there's one place the loop hides better than anywhere else:

Inside success.

10 Insider Tactics to Escape the B.R.E.A.K. Loop (Before It Starts)

These tactics come from books, tutorials, videos, and the occasional private group. I've collected what works—not what's trendy—to give you tools you can apply right now, before you're funded. Some are overlooked. A few are even a little gray hat.

1. "Future Me" Trade Review Trick

After each session, record a voice note **as your future self—6 months ahead—reviewing your behavior today.**
Traders doing this often stop self-sabotage in its tracks. Why? It creates a time-jump in perspective, detaching you from today's ego-driven noise.

> *This method is quietly used in elite trading prop desks to instill "legacy identity" into recruits.*

2. Trade Entry = Triggered Affirmation Hack
(Gray Hat Neuroscience)

Every time you hit "Buy" or "Sell," **trigger a short script in your head or aloud:**
"This trade doesn't define me. My process does."
This uses **anchoring + operant conditioning** to rewire the high-stress association with trade execution.

3. Inverted Mentorship Sessions

Once per week, do a "Bad Trade Breakdown"—**but pretend you're coaching a new trader through your exact mistake.**

Seeing your behavior through a mentor lens creates rapid awareness and cognitive dissonance—two key pattern breakers.

> Pro desks have entire team rituals built around this. It rewires identity faster than solo journaling.

4. Pattern Break Desk Setup

Rearrange your physical desk **every time you hit 3 emotional trades in a row.**
Even swapping monitors, chair angles, or lighting creates psychological friction. This disrupts automated behavior loops and forces renewed attention.

> Gray Hat Tactic: Some traders go as far as changing mouse hands or screen colors during tilt periods to force a new mental pattern.

5. Cognitive Cost Calculator

Before switching a strategy, create and fill out a "Switch Cost Form" with:

- Time to retrain muscle memory
- Risk of false confidence
- Opportunity cost of mastery delay
- This is used in behavioral finance coaching to slow impulsive pivoting—key in halting the **"K" in B.R.E.A.K. (Keep Switching).**

6. Post-Trade Identity Casting

After each win or loss, write one line about **what this trade says about the kind of trader you're becoming.**

Not the setup. Not the result. But the identity signal. You'll spot "identity drift" long before it wrecks your system.

7. "Break-the-Loop" Alarm System

Set an alarm mid-session titled:

> "Are you trading the plan—or your emotion right now?"
> This jolts System 2 online at the peak point of potential reactivity. It's a micro-intervention pulled from addiction recovery cue-disruption techniques.

8. Strategy Graveyard Archive

Create a private doc or Notion board of **all strategies you've abandoned.** Include:

- Why you started
- Why you left

Review it monthly. This triggers pattern recognition and helps kill strategy-hopping addiction by confronting your "escape data."

9. The "Loss Avatar" Exercise *(Advanced Psychology Trick)*

Draw or describe the *persona* of your worst self as a trader. Name it. Give it traits.

Example: "Rage Randy - jumps in after losses, doubles size, needs to win back respect."

This creates emotional distance from the behavior, so you can observe it instead of being hijacked by it.

10. Boredom as Alpha Drill

Once per week, **sit at the charts during your normal session window—but commit to not trading unless an A+ setup appears.**

This rewires your brain to normalize boredom and detach from urgency. Many funded traders use this to train "presence without activity"—an underused edge.

Final Thought

You don't break loops with knowledge. You break them with **disruptive identity design.** These hacks are about rewiring the emotional reflexes that trap traders for months—or years.

> If Chapter 1 was the mirror, Chapter 2 is the jackhammer. Now you've got the tools to smash through the loop.

In Chapter 3, we dive into the **paradox of being funded**—how passing a challenge isn't the same as being ready, why performance under pressure reveals your true trading identity, and how external funding can either expose your growth or magnify your weaknesses.

If you think the pressure ends when you get funded—you're in for a brutal surprise.

But if you're ready to trade like a professional—not just get paid like one—then Chapter 3 is your next mission.

Let's go.

CHAPTER 3

The Funded Illusion

The Funded Fantasy

The Funded Fantasy
Getting funded feels like a dream. You've passed the challenge. You beat the metrics. You wake up to that email: "Congratulations, you are now a funded trader." You tell your friends. You post the screenshot. You imagine payouts, freedom, scaling up. You feel like a pro.

And right there—**that feeling is the trap**.

Because passing a challenge isn't becoming a pro. It's performing well in a controlled environment. A funded account isn't a prize. It's a pressure test.

The fantasy is that funding equals transformation. That somehow, the moment you get access to capital, you'll become more focused, more consistent, more "professional."

But in reality? Capital doesn't upgrade you. **It amplifies who you already are.**

The Lottery Winner Curse

Ever heard of lottery winners going broke in a year?

It happens all the time. Why? Because they got the money, but not the *mindset*. The internal system didn't match the external reward.

Same thing in trading. You passed the challenge, but if your process is shaky, your identity still reactive, and your rules still optional—you'll treat that funded account like a scratch-off win. You'll overtrade, chase, panic, and lose.

Because it's not about getting the capital. It's about becoming the kind of person who can **sustain** it.

You don't need to be lucky to get funded. You need to be stable to keep it.

Performance vs. Proof

Prop firm challenges test **performance**. Real trading demands **proof**.

Performance is short-term. It's burst energy, a highlight reel, a sprint. You can hit a lucky streak. You can game the system.

Proof is different. Proof is boring. It's consistent execution over time. It's patience under stress. It's making peace with small gains and routine habits.

Passing the challenge is your audition. Staying funded is your career.

Don't confuse one with the other.

The Trap of Validation

After getting funded, a lot of traders start trading for the wrong audience.

You start thinking about what others will say. You want to prove you deserved it. You want to impress your mentor. Or flex on Twitter. Or post the payout.

That need for external validation corrupts your execution. You start taking trades for ego, not edge.

Validation is a drug. The more you chase it, the more reactive you become. And nothing wrecks a funded account faster than needing to be right all the time.

Let go of the audience. Trade for your future, not their approval.

Screenshot Ego Addiction

Let's talk about it.

You get one good payout. One clean trade. You screenshot it. You feel like a boss. You want to feel it again—so you size up. You skip steps. You chase the high, not the habit.

You start living off the memory of a great day. But trading doesn't care about yesterday.

Screenshots are souvenirs. They feel good, but they don't make you consistent. The real game is in the trades no one sees. The boring ones. The rule-based ones. The ones that don't impress, but *compound*.

If your ego needs a screenshot to feel validated, you're not trading—you're performing.

Confusing Capital with Skill

Here's the hardest pill: getting funded doesn't mean you're skilled.

It means you completed a task. A challenge with defined rules and limits. Good job. But that's not the same as *mastery*.

Capital can make you feel smarter than you are. But money in the account is just a number. What matters is how you handle it under pressure.

A trader with skill can take a $5k account and grow it slowly. A trader without skill can blow $100k in a week. Capital without maturity is just risk wearing a suit.

The Prop Firm Paradox

The Prop Firm Paradox

Here's something most traders don't realize until it's too late:

Prop firms aren't just trying to fund traders. They're trying to **filter** them.

Think about it. They know most people won't last. They're not betting on your success—they're observing your process. The real test doesn't end at the challenge. It *starts* the moment you're funded.

And the paradox? The challenge trains you for the **wrong battle**.

Passing Without Mastery

You can pass a prop challenge without real discipline.

- You can get lucky on a news event.
- You can catch one strong week.
- You can size up and pass in 5 trades.

But none of that proves you're consistent. None of that tests how you handle boredom. Or drawdown. Or a losing week.

Passing proves you're good in a **controlled environment**. But staying funded requires emotional control in an *unstructured battlefield.*

The challenge rewards precision under rules. Real trading punishes emotion under pressure.

Why Most Traders Fail Post-Funding

Let's be blunt: the majority of traders who get funded will lose it.

Not because they suddenly got worse—but because everything around them changed:

- The pressure to perform is higher.
- The emotional stake is real.
- The safety net is gone.

Now, your behavior matters more than ever.

Before, a 3% drawdown was just data. Now it feels like failure. Before, you could swing for a pass. Now, you're managing capital—and emotion.

Most traders fail not due to strategy. They fail because they can't **stabilize themselves** in a higher-stakes environment.

Risk Compression Anxiety

Here's a term you won't hear often: **risk compression**.

It's what happens when traders go from demoing or simulating a challenge—where they take risks freely—to a funded account where every trade "counts."

Suddenly, they start under-risking. They get scared. They pass on good trades. They don't let setups breathe. Or worse—they over-risk trying to make up for all the hesitation.

You're compressing your edge into a fear box. The math is still there—but your emotions shrink it.

The irony? The fear of losing makes you behave in ways that increase the chances you'll lose.

Changing Behavior Under Pressure

Same strategy. Same rules. But now you're funded—and suddenly, you're acting different.

You hesitate on clean trades. You exit too early. You avoid setups that worked last month.

What changed?

Not the market. You.

Pressure triggers identity regression. You go from the calm, focused trader back to the one who second-guesses and seeks safety.

The problem isn't pressure—it's your relationship with pressure.

If you don't train for high-stakes situations, you'll default to your lowest habit the moment tension rises.

External Goal, Internal Chaos

The goal was always clear: *Get funded.* That gave you structure, discipline, urgency.

But the moment you reach the goal… what happens?

You lose your target. You lose your framework. And suddenly, you're left with internal chaos.

Now there's no scoreboard. No deadline. No external mission.

And if you don't create a new one—your mind will. It'll start chasing dopamine. Needing to win. Needing to prove.

That's the fastest way to burn out your edge.

The solution? Replace the external goal with an internal one: *Trade like a pro. Every day. Whether anyone is watching or not.*

Real Funding, Real Pressure

The Psychological Cost of Capital

Here's the thing they don't tell you when they sell you the dream:

Capital isn't free. It comes with psychological weight.

When you finally get access to a larger account, you don't just get opportunity—you get emotional leverage.

You feel every tick more. Every mistake louder. Every small drawdown heavier.

It's no longer hypothetical. Now it's *real money*. It doesn't matter if it's technically the prop firm's capital—your nervous system doesn't know that. Your nervous system thinks: *Don't screw this up.*

And once you start thinking like that? You're not trading anymore. You're protecting. And that protection creates tension. That tension creates reactive decisions.

Capital gives you scale. But if your mindset isn't ready, all it does is **amplify stress**.

Funding = Amplifier of Habits

Let's make something clear: money doesn't fix bad habits.

It **magnifies** them.

If you were impulsive on a $5K demo, you'll be impulsive on a $100K funded account—just faster and with more consequences.

Capital is like a loudspeaker. It doesn't change your message. It just broadcasts it louder.

That's why so many traders blow their first funded accounts. Because they were hoping money would *make* them a pro. Instead, it just revealed that they're still thinking like an amateur.

The capital is not the reward. The capital is the **mirror**.

Mental Fragility Under Review

Here's a unique twist of prop firm life: you're being watched.

Every trade you take is reviewed. Every drawdown measured. Every stat tracked. It's not just the money—it's the feeling of being *judged*.

And that creates **mental fragility**.

You start second-guessing yourself. You avoid creative trades. You fear disqualification. You hesitate—not because the trade is bad, but because you don't want to look bad.

You're no longer trading for the system. You're trading for approval. And that approval mindset weakens your edge.

Strong traders execute. Fragile traders overthink.

You need to protect your **mental flexibility**—or you'll become a robot under pressure.

The Accountability Shock

Before funding, it's easy to say "I'm disciplined." Easy to journal. Easy to follow your rules when the only one affected is you.

But once you're funded?

Now your decisions impact *real* equity. Now your risk manager can cut your account. Now every decision has an audience—even if it's just your own expectations.

That's when accountability hits. And for many traders, it's a shock.

They realize they weren't truly accountable before—they were just *unconfronted*. The funded account brings it all to the surface.

You either rise to that level of responsibility—or you collapse under it.

Why Rules Feel Like Prisons

Here's the paradox: the rules you loved during the challenge—the ones that gave you structure, the ones that helped you stay focused—now feel restrictive.

You start thinking:

- "I could've taken that if I didn't have the daily loss limit."
- "I hate having to use stop-losses that tight."
- "These prop firm rules are holding me back."

But here's the truth:

The rules aren't the problem. Your desire to bypass them is.

Rules don't limit you. They define you. They keep your behavior consistent when your emotions want chaos.

When rules start to feel like prisons, it's a sign your ego is trying to escape accountability.

Freedom in trading doesn't come from fewer rules. It comes from the discipline to follow the ones that protect your edge—even when they're inconvenient.

Identity Rewire

The Pre-Funded Mind Game

Most traders think the real test starts after they're funded.

But the truth is — the test started *long* before that. It started in the hours no one saw. In the way you journaled. In how you reacted to a losing day. In whether you traded bored… or didn't trade at all.

The pre-funded phase is where your identity was being trained. Or not.

And if you skipped that inner work? Getting funded won't fill the gap. It will just **expose it**.

The pressure of funding doesn't forge your discipline — it reveals whether you already had any.

Identity Scripts: Trader vs. Gambler

Here's a hard truth: most traders aren't actually traders. They're gamblers with good vocabulary.

- The trader has rules. The gambler has hopes.
- The trader follows process. The gambler follows emotion.
- The trader embraces boredom. The gambler needs excitement.

So ask yourself: who are you in your average trading day?

Do you log your setups before entry? Do you take losses without revenge? Do you stop after a red day and regroup?

Or do you chase, flip pairs, size up, and pray?

The market doesn't care what you call yourself. It only responds to **behavior**. And if your behavior is impulsive, erratic, and emotional — then you're not a trader. You're a high-functioning slot machine addict with a trading platform.

It's time to rewrite your script.

Replacing the Hope Trade with the Habit Trade

Hope is a beautiful thing. But in trading? It's a killer.

Hope trades sound like:

- "This might work."
- "Maybe it bounces here."
- "I just need one good run."

Habit trades sound like:

- "This is my setup."
- "This fits my plan."
- "This is the same execution I've drilled 50 times."

Hope trades are driven by emotion. Habit trades are driven by repetition. Hope feels exciting. Habit feels boring.

But here's the magic: **boring is profitable.**

The more boring your trades feel, the more professional you're becoming. Consistency lives in repetition — not thrill.

Identity Before Results

This is the core principle of this entire chapter:

> You don't become a consistent trader *after* the results show up. You become one when you start acting like the trader who *deserves* those results.

Most people get this backward. They wait to feel like a pro. They wait to feel confident. They wait until the equity curve validates them.

But identity works the other way around. You decide who you are. Then you align your behavior to that identity.

And over time? The market starts to reflect it.

Trading isn't just a numbers game. It's a **who are you when it gets hard** game. That's identity. That's edge.

The One-Sentence Identity Technique

Let's make it simple.

Write one sentence that defines the trader you want to become. Not some vision board fluff — something real. Something you can read daily before you trade.

Examples:

- "I am a focused, funded trader who executes cleanly and protects capital with discipline."
- "I don't trade for dopamine — I trade for longevity."
- "I act like the pro I'm becoming, not the amateur I used to be."

Say it out loud. Print it. Post it. Repeat it until it becomes reflex.

Your identity is your anchor. When things get shaky, come back to it. Let that sentence override the voice of your old self. Because that voice — the one that panics, chases, and breaks rules — will show up.

But if your identity is strong enough, it won't win.

Build the Trader Before the Funding

"You Don't Get Funded to Trade Like a Pro. You Trade Like a Pro to Get Funded."

That line?

It's not just clever. It's everything.

It flips the illusion. It burns down the fantasy. And it forces you to ask the one question that actually matters:

"Am I already acting like the trader I claim to be?"

Because if you're still waiting for funding to *make* you professional... it won't. If you're hoping that capital will create discipline, or that a payout will give you confidence—you're already behind.

The pro mindset doesn't arrive when the account does. It **precedes it**. It's the cause, not the result.

You Trade Into the Identity

Getting funded is just another external event. It can't give you what you haven't already built internally.

Professionals don't flip a switch once they pass Phase 2. They don't get more serious because the capital is bigger. They show up the same **before, during**, and **after**. Calm. Clean. Clear. Committed.

They were already funded in their process long before the email came.

The Rookie Mistake

The amateur thinks, *"Once I get the account, I'll level up."*

That mindset is why they blow it.

Because the moment something goes wrong—and it will—your old patterns show up. Not because you're bad, but because you haven't **rewired** who you are.

- You still chase the next trade.
- You still avoid your journal.
- You still click when you're anxious.
- You still think the next trade is the one that'll fix everything.

You don't need more leverage. You need more **emotional leverage** over your habits.

The Professional Approach

The pro isn't perfect. They're not robotic. But they are grounded.

- They know their edge.
- They protect their capital.
- They stay emotionally neutral.
- They trade with purpose, not proof.

And most importantly, they understand this:

> The game doesn't start when you get funded.
> It starts when you stop needing funding to validate your identity.

This Isn't About Funding

Here's the real twist:

This chapter was never really about prop firms. Or funded accounts. Or passing challenges.

It was about **you.**

Your behavior. Your decisions. Your discipline.

Funding is just a magnifier. It exposes the truth you've been carrying into every trade.

So now ask yourself:

- Are you showing up like a funded trader right now?
- Or are you still waiting for something external to force you into maturity?

One of those roads leads to growth. The other leads to collapse.

You don't get funded to trade like a pro. You trade like a pro… and that's why you get funded.

So stop asking for capital.

Start asking for accountability.

That's the real currency. That's the real shift.

10 Elite-Level Tactics to Survive (and Thrive) After Getting Funded

These tactics weren't invented by me—they were collected. I've found them in trading books, deep-dive tutorials, YouTube videos, and the occasional private group or paid course. Some are well-hidden, others are just underused—but together, they form a playbook of practical, powerful ways to upgrade how you trade.

1. "Audit Mode" Overlay

Install a *browser extension or trade journal interface* that overlays the phrase:

> **"You are under audit."**
> on your chart window.
> This mimics the **perception of surveillance**, reducing sloppy execution. Behavioral studies show we act 20–40% more aligned with rules when we feel watched—even if it's artificial.
>
> *Prop firms don't just watch for violations. They psychologically expect you to self-correct.*

2. Inverse Screenshot Rule

For every screenshot-worthy win you post or save, you must also document one **boring, non-screenshot trade** that followed all your rules but didn't look impressive.
This rewires your reward system to seek **consistency > clout**, breaking the *screenshot ego addiction.*

3. "Drawdown Day Ritual" (Used by funded pros in stealth)

Pre-plan a ritual that triggers **only on red days**—example:

- 3-mile walk
- Ice bath
- Voice note review

Why? It teaches your body and brain that *losing = reset,* not revenge. Most elite traders don't avoid red days—they *train their nervous system* to metabolize them fast.

4. Trade Like You're Managing OPM

Pretend your funded capital is **client money**, not firm money. Use an "OPM Overlay" mental model:

> "Would I still take this trade if I had to explain it to a boardroom of investors tomorrow morning?" This is an old hedge fund trick for stabilizing impulse trading.

5. The "5 Trade Cooldown" Protocol

If you pass a challenge in under 5 trades, you're on emotional fire. Cooldown before going live.
The protocol:

- 5 micro-size trades at full process quality
- No capital goals
- Only journal and execution grading
- Used by quant desks to re-ground hot streak traders before they deploy real size.

6. "Post-Funding Blindfold" Drill

For your first 3 funded days, **turn off your equity and PnL display.** This rewires you to **trade the chart, not the cash.** Many pros run this as a filter to see how deep emotional attachment runs. If your process breaks without visible numbers—you're not ready for size.

7. Reverse Lottery Visualization

Every morning, visualize the *worst funded outcome*:

> "If I blew this account in 3 trades, what identity would I regress to?"
> Then visualize *that identity watching you trade.*
> This gray hat tactic flips the emotional reward system—replacing "don't screw it up" with "trade clean because you're already watched by your failure ghost."

8. Public Process Proofing (Mini Accountability Injection)

Share your **trade process, not your results**, in a private accountability group or to a trusted coach/peer:

- Pre-trade checklist
- Emotional rating
- Screenshot + journal snippet
- This inoculates you from **performing for PnL**, which is where most funded traders implode.

9. The "Mentor Cam" Drill

Record your live screen (OBS or Loom) and imagine your *future pro self* is watching.

You won't overtrade. You won't skip rituals.
Some funded traders go so far as to **pretend they're live streaming to a hedge fund mentor**. It forces peak behavior—even in silence.

10. Identity-First Risk Scaling

Don't scale your lot size based on success.
Scale it based on identity milestones:

- "I've journaled 20 trades without deviation."
- "I've followed rules 3 weeks straight, even during drawdown."
- This builds emotional congruency with capital growth. Scaling without identity creates the illusion of control—which evaporates under pressure.

Final Word

Getting funded is **not the test**—it's the mirror. These hacks are designed to keep your identity sharp when the fantasy wears off and the pressure kicks in.

> **Funding doesn't make you ready. Funding shows if you already were.**

In chapter 4, we'll break down exactly why willpower isn't enough, why motivation always fails under market pressure, and how traders can build unshakable daily rituals that don't rely on "feeling like it."

If Chapter 3 exposed the illusion—Chapter 4 gives you the armor to never fall for it again.

CHAPTER 4

Emotional Rigging – How FOMO, Fear, and Revenge Trading Hijack You

Section 1: The FOMO Trigger System

FOMO isn't a trading issue. It's a **nervous system issue**. It's your brain reacting to perceived danger—only the "danger" is missing out on a trade that's already moving.

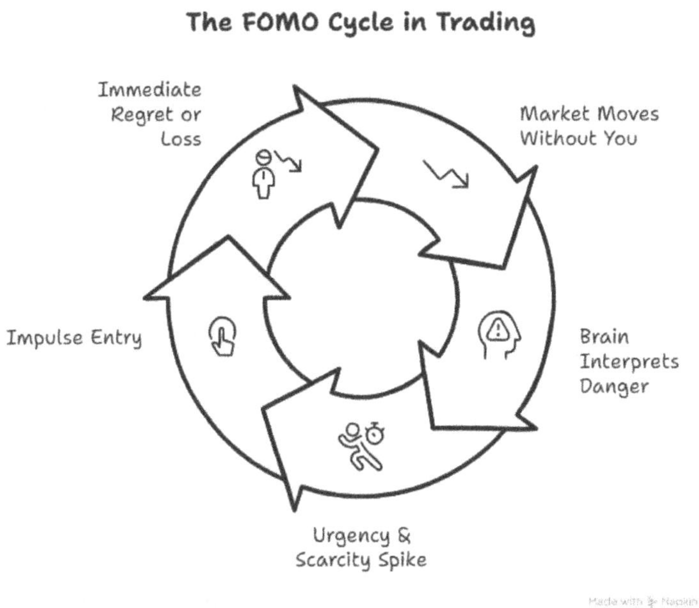

It feels like adrenaline. It sounds like urgency. It shows up in your thoughts like:

- "If I don't catch this, I'll fall behind."
- "Everyone else is in this—why am I not?"
- "This could be *the* move."

But none of that is logic. It's **emotional hijacking**. And it starts a loop that sabotages even the best traders.

The Siren Song of Certainty

FOMO whispers one dangerous promise: **"This time, it's obvious."**

That's the bait.

The candle is surging. Volume is up. It *looks* clean. So you abandon your checklist. You ignore the entry rules. You jump in late because you "just know."

But what you're chasing isn't a setup. You're chasing **certainty**. And certainty is a lie in trading. By the time it feels obvious, it's often already over.

Professional traders know that certainty is a feeling—not a signal. If it feels too easy, too obvious, too perfect—it's probably a trap.

Social Media and the Scarcity Loop

Let's be honest: social media fuels your FOMO.

You scroll through stories of funded traders, payout screenshots, "caught the move" videos. You're watching the highlight reels of people you don't even know—filtered, curated, performance-driven.

This triggers the **scarcity loop**:

> "They're winning. I'm not. Time is running out. I need to catch up."

Suddenly, you're not trading anymore. You're chasing someone else's timeline. Someone else's results. And that's a race you will always lose—because it's not your race.

The solution? Starve the loop. Take breaks from social feeds before sessions. Replace dopamine scrolling with mental prep. The market isn't going anywhere. Your clarity? That's what's actually rare.

Overtrading as Dopamine Addiction

Overtrading isn't about strategy. It's about **state**.

Each click gives you a hit. A rush. Even losing trades deliver a surge of chemical stimulation. And your brain learns, *"This feels good. Do it again."*

It's not that you're stupid. You're literally running on a **dopamine loop**.

The more you feed it, the more you crave it. And soon, you're not looking for clean trades—you're looking for **any trade**. You're not building an account. You're building a habit of chaos.

Trading has to be boring to be profitable. But if you're trading for stimulation, boredom feels like death. And so you chase. And click. And bleed.

The real pros? They're addicted to **discipline**, not dopamine.

Missed Trade Syndrome

Let's talk about that sinking feeling when you watch a trade run without you. You had it marked. It was in your zone. You hesitated… and now it's gone.

You feel regret. You feel stupid. You feel like the market just *proved* you're not good enough.

That's **Missed Trade Syndrome.**

And here's what happens next:

- You force the next trade.
- You trade subpar setups to make up for "missing it."
- You emotionally double-down on the next signal—even if it's trash.

All because you made the **most human mistake**: thinking that one trade defines you.

Missing a trade isn't failure. Chasing the next one out of guilt? That's the real error.

Train yourself to bless missed trades. Say, "Good. My plan said no. I'm still in control." Because the more you can *let go,* the more the market will come to you.

Impulse vs. Intuition

Here's where things get tricky: sometimes you *feel* the trade before it forms. You sense the setup. You anticipate the flow.

Is that intuition? Or is it impulse?

The difference is simple:

- **Intuition is quiet.** It's grounded in experience. It respects your plan.
- **Impulse is loud.** It's emotional. It demands urgency. It doesn't care about rules.

Traders confuse the two all the time. They say, "I just knew," when really, they just reacted.

You want intuition? Earn it. Build pattern recognition. Rehearse your process. Review your journals. The more data your brain has logged through repetition, the more it can spot opportunity without panic.

Intuition is the reward for patience. Impulse is the punishment for skipping process.

Section 2: Fear-Based Paralysis

Fear doesn't always show up as panic. Sometimes, it shows up as silence. As freezing. As **doing nothing** when your system says go.

And that's the killer most traders never see coming—not failure, but **paralysis.**

The Fear of Losing

The most obvious fear. You enter a trade and immediately imagine it hitting stop-loss. You tighten your SL. You size down. You hesitate.

You're not trading to win—you're trading to *avoid pain.*

This fear creates passive behavior. You miss clean setups, or worse—cut trades too early to "lock in" a tiny gain.

Here's the truth: **losing is part of the game.** You cannot trade without it. But fearing losses guarantees you'll take more of them.

When you fear a loss, you shrink your edge. You interfere with the process. You sabotage your own math.

The best traders? They lose **flawlessly.** No panic. No drama. Just data.

The Fear of Missing

This is FOMO's quieter sibling.

You're afraid the move is going to happen *without* you. So you enter early. Or late. You skip confirmation. You jump on the "almost" setup.

You'd rather be *in* the market than risk being left out.

But the irony? Acting from the fear of missing is the fastest way to **miss consistently.**

Because you'll always be slightly off. Slightly too soon. Slightly too desperate.

Instead of flowing with your strategy, you're front-running the market. And the market smells desperation like blood in the water.

Let the move go. Let the candle close. Let your system lead.

If it runs without you? Good. You stayed in control. That's a win.

The Fear of Being Wrong

This fear is sneakier than the others. It doesn't feel like panic—it feels like ego.

You want to be right. You *need* to be right. So you avoid losses. You avoid risk. You avoid any setup that doesn't feel "perfect."

You're no longer trading to follow your system. You're trading to **protect your identity**.

And when the market challenges you? You double down. You move your stop. You hold a loser because you "know it's gonna reverse."

You're not afraid of the red. You're afraid of the story it tells: *"Maybe you're not good at this."*

But being wrong is part of being a trader. What matters isn't avoiding it—it's **how quickly you correct.**

Professionals aren't afraid of being wrong. They're afraid of letting ego dig the hole deeper.

Risk Aversion as Self-Sabotage

Risk management is essential. But **excessive risk aversion** is a form of self-sabotage.

You lower your size so much that even your wins don't matter. You pass on setups because they "feel risky." You keep waiting for a perfect moment that never comes.

You're not protecting your capital. You're avoiding responsibility.

The market rewards exposure to controlled risk. If you're never uncomfortable, you're probably never positioned to grow.

Ask yourself: *Am I being smart? Or scared?*

Because fear dressed up as caution is still fear.

Most fear doesn't show up as screaming panic—it whispers in the form of fake logic.

"This setup doesn't feel quite right."

"Let's wait for more confirmation."

But under the hood? It's fear pretending to be wisdom. Your job is to learn the difference between rational caution and emotional avoidance.

Hesitation Kills More Trades Than Mistakes

Let's be real: hesitation is the silent killer.

You see the setup. You've marked it. It's in your plan.

But instead of entering, you wait. You second-guess. You switch timeframes. You look for more "confirmation" that's really just emotional reassurance.

And by the time you act? It's too late.

Hesitation doesn't feel like failure. It feels "safe." But every time you hesitate on a valid trade, you're training your brain to **doubt your system**.

It chips away at confidence. It turns clean setups into confusion. And eventually? You stop taking trades entirely.

Here's the truth: **it's better to lose on a clean setup than miss it because of fear.** At least then, you're reinforcing process.

Take the shot. Let the outcome be what it is. Confidence is built through action—not through avoidance.

Section 3: Revenge Trading & Tilt

Most traders think their worst losses come from bad analysis.

They don't.

They come from revenge. From tilt. From that emotional swing where you go from *disciplined executor* to *panicked clicker*. Where every trade becomes a desperate attempt to get back what you just lost.

This isn't trading. This is emotional combustion.

The Emotional Explosion

You take a clean trade. It hits stop-loss. You're annoyed.

Then another one. It loses again. Now you're angry.

And then it happens—the switch flips.

Your heart rate spikes. Your breathing shortens. Your screen becomes an enemy. You feel like something's been *taken* from you. And all you want is to take it **back.**

So you re-enter.

Not because it fits your plan. But because you can't sit with the feeling of being down.

That's not strategy. That's emotional debt collection.

And the market does not pay emotional debts. It **charges interest**.

The Fight/Flight/FOMO Spiral

When you hit tilt, your body enters survival mode. Literally.

Your brain floods with cortisol. Your frontal lobe (the decision-maker) shuts down. And your primal brain takes over.

Now you're in one of three modes:

- **Fight:** You double down. You size up. You force setups to "win it back."
- **Flight:** You avoid re-entering altogether. You stare at charts and stew in silence.
- **FOMO:** You switch pairs. You hunt for something—*anything*—to trade.

You're no longer in control. Your biology is. And it's making trading decisions based on fear, not function.

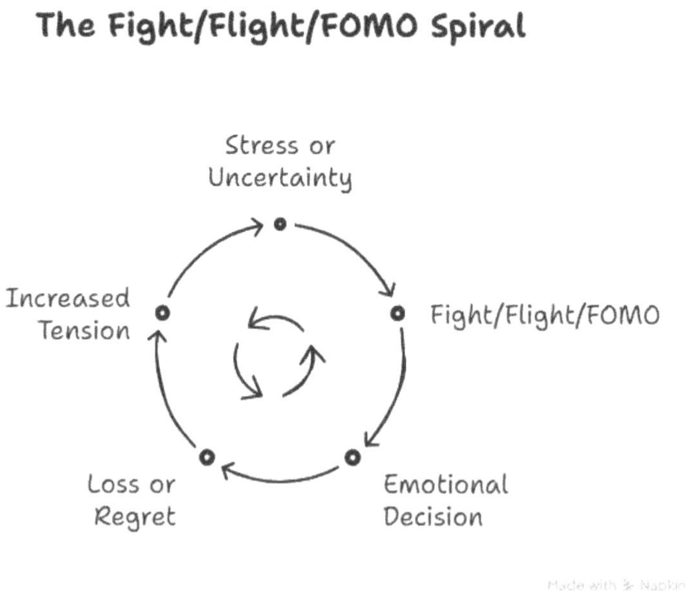

Overcorrection Errors

This is the trap that comes right after a revenge spiral:

You overcorrect.

You go from clicking everything to clicking nothing. You freeze. You avoid valid trades because you "don't trust yourself." You lower size to the point that wins feel meaningless.

Or worse—you start breaking every rule trying to *make up for* the meltdown.

It's like driving into a skid and yanking the wheel too far the other way. You don't fix the problem—you just crash on the other side.

Recovery doesn't come from swinging back hard. It comes from slowing down, stabilizing, and **re-centering on process.**

From Data to Drama

When you're in tilt mode, you stop seeing setups. You start seeing stories.

- "This pair always screws me."
- "The market's out to get me."
- "This was manipulated."
- "I *have* to win this one."

Now you're not using data anymore. You're trading **narratives.** And narratives are dangerous, because they justify emotional decisions. They make it feel *logical* to act irrationally.

This is the moment you need to step away. Not for five minutes. For the day. Because if you keep trading, you're not fixing the problem—you're feeding it.

Discipline Meltdowns

Revenge trading doesn't just kill your PnL. It kills your **identity** as a trader.

You spend weeks building discipline. Routines. Journals. Self-trust.

And one revenge spiral nukes it all.

The next time you sit down to trade, part of you remembers: *"I lost control."* That memory sticks. And now, even your clean trades are shadowed by hesitation or self-doubt.

The meltdown doesn't end when the red trade closes. It ends when you rebuild the mindset that you **broke.**

And that takes time. Humility. Patience. And a deep willingness to forgive yourself—but never excuse the behavior.

Section 4: Detachment Systems

Let's face it — emotions aren't going away. You can't trade without fear, greed, or doubt creeping in. But what you can do is build systems that make you emotionally bulletproof. Systems that create enough space between you and your feelings so you can actually trade with clarity.

This is what detachment is about. Not becoming robotic. Not becoming cold. But learning how to feel everything… and act on none of it unless it aligns with your plan.

One of the best mindset drills I ever did had nothing to do with charts. It was when I ran three marathons in three days with my friend Justin. Around Vilnius, Lithuania, a 100km hiking trail had just opened, wrapping through forests, riversides, and historic paths around the city. We thought, "Why not run it?" So we split it into three days—42km on day one, 42km on day two, and with just 16km left on the final day, we added a few more kilometers just to make it a clean 126km. Three marathons in three days. Not because we had to. But because it trained the part of us that refuses to quit.

There were no extreme weather conditions, but there were plenty of moments when Uber looked tempting. That was the real training. Detaching from short-term comfort. Choosing completion over convenience. It's the same in trading. When things get boring or tough, the temptation is to "Uber out"—to break the rules, cut corners, chase action. But the best traders, like the best runners, build a mindset that says, "I'm finishing this—no matter what."

Let's build that same mindset—through detachment, discipline, and deliberate systems. Here are 3 strong tips to help you build the same kind of resilient, detachment-powered mindset:

1. Practice Discomfort on Purpose

Don't wait for the market to challenge you—train yourself to embrace discomfort in controlled environments. Take cold showers. Fast for 16 hours. Run when you don't feel like it. These aren't about health or fitness—they're about proving to your brain that you can act without needing comfort. The more often you lean into discomfort by choice, the easier it becomes to stay calm and deliberate when discomfort shows up in trading.

2. Journal Your Emotion-Triggers Like a Scientist

After each session, rate your emotional stability (1–10), and document what thoughts or feelings tried to hijack you. Were you anxious because you were down? Bored and wanted to click something? Recognize the patterns. If you can name your triggers, you can tame them. The goal is not emotional elimination—it's emotional awareness with distance.

3. Delay Every Decision by 60 Seconds

Every time you feel the urge to enter, exit, or adjust a trade, pause for 60 seconds. Breathe. Re-read your trading rules. Ask: "Is this part of my plan—or part of my panic?" That one-minute pause is a mental gym rep. It builds a reflex of control, a buffer zone between feeling and action. Over time, that pause becomes a superpower.

These practices harden your mindset not just for trading—but for life.

Trading Zen Mode

"Zen" isn't a buzzword here. It's a trading **state**.

Zen Mode means slowing the mind before you enter the charts. No urgency. No "need" to trade. Just observation, breathing, and clarity.

Think of it as putting your brain in **scan mode**, not **hunt mode**.

Ways to enter Zen Mode:

- 5 minutes of stillness before your session
- A short breathing routine (inhale 4, hold 4, exhale 4)
- Reviewing your plan like a ritual, not a checklist

When you start in Zen, you trade from *neutral.* That's where high-quality execution lives.

Silent Chart Sessions

Not every session has to include a trade.

In fact, some of your most important growth will happen in sessions where you **don't click at all.**

Silent sessions are where you observe, mark up, note behavior — but you don't enter. You let the market move without you. You train your nervous system to be okay with *not participating.*

This builds detachment like nothing else.

It rewires your brain from:

> "I need to trade to prove I'm doing something" to
> "I'm improving just by watching."

And that mindset shift? It creates insane patience when the real setup comes.

Intentional Discomfort Exposure

Want to trade better under pressure? You need to build tolerance for **discomfort** outside the charts.

Because if your brain only feels "safe" when everything is calm, the first red candle will wreck you.

Here's how to train your mind:

- Cold showers (builds pain tolerance + emotional reset)
- Early wake-ups (builds grit + mental clarity)
- Daily exercise (releases stress + strengthens identity)
- Social discomfort (having hard conversations, saying "no")

These small, physical challenges bleed into trading. They tell your nervous system, *"We can handle tension without panic."*

Discomfort in your day = calm under the candles.

Pain-Reward Rituals

Every time you lose a trade or make a mistake, you're at a fork:

- Beat yourself up
- Or **retrain your response**

Pain is inevitable in trading. But how you respond to it? That's what shapes your future.

Create a *ritual* around it.

Example:

- After a loss, write a one-line journal entry: *"I followed my system, the result doesn't define me."*
- Or: *"I broke rule #3. Next time I will pause and breathe."*

- Then reward yourself with something neutral — like stepping away and taking a walk, or marking the trade as "logged" and moving on.

This builds emotional closure. It stops you from spiraling. And it reinforces that your **behavior**, not your outcome, is what defines a good trader.

Trading Like a Stoic Samurai

Think of the greatest warriors in history — calm, deliberate, in control.

They didn't draw their sword out of emotion. They moved with clarity and readiness.

That's the energy you want in trading.

- Prepare your plan like a warrior sharpens a blade.
- Sit in silence like a sniper in position.
- Strike only when your system says so — not your feelings.

A Stoic Samurai trader doesn't avoid emotion. He just doesn't serve it.

He trades by principle, not pressure. And that's why he survives when others melt down.

Section 5: Takeaway Principle

"You Can't Outperform the Market If You Can't Outlast Your Emotions."

Here's the truth that breaks most traders before the market ever does:

It's not your system.
It's not your win rate.
It's not your tools.

It's your *emotional tolerance.*

You could have the best strategy on the planet—but if your brain short-circuits the second you take a loss, or the moment a candle moves against you… it doesn't matter.

Your edge gets hijacked. Your logic gets silenced. Your habits collapse.

And now you're not trading anymore. You're reacting.

Emotions Are Part of the Game — But Not the Strategy

You will feel fear.
You will feel greed.
You will want revenge.
You will want to jump in early, exit too late, or double your size.

That's normal.

The goal is not emotional perfection. That doesn't exist. The goal is emotional **durability** — to feel everything and still execute cleanly.

You trade better than most? Great.

Now trade better than your *worst moments.*

That's the real test.

You Don't Rise to Your Plan — You Fall to Your State

You could have the cleanest strategy in the world. But when pressure hits? You won't rise to it. You'll fall to the level of your preparation, your routines, and your **emotional baseline.**

If you don't train for those moments—FOMO will win.

Fear will win.

Tilt will win.

And the worst part? You'll think the market beat you. But it wasn't the market. It was your reaction to it.

We all know the emotional spike after a loss. But what about the post-win fog? The moment after a big green day when you start forcing setups to 'keep the streak alive'? That's just as dangerous. You're chasing a feeling, not a signal.

The Traders Who Last...

They're not superhuman. They just don't treat emotions as truth. They treat them like **weather**—it comes, it passes, it doesn't decide the plan.

They don't try to eliminate emotion. They train to trade *through* it.

That's what detachment looks like. That's what builds consistency. That's what separates the professionals from the potential.

Final Thought

You will never escape your emotions. But you can outlast them.

And when you do, you stop sabotaging your edge. You stop reacting to noise. You start trading with clarity—even in chaos.

The market doesn't require perfection.
But it demands resilience.

Train for that.

10 Insider Tactics to Master FOMO, Fear, and Tilt Before They Hijack You

These tactics come from books, tutorials, videos, and the occasional private group. I've collected what works—not what's trendy—to give you tools you can apply right now, before you're funded. Some are overlooked. A few are even a little gray hat.

1. The "Emotion Trigger Map"

Create a personal **trading trigger map** of *where* specific emotions tend to hijack you.
Example:

- FOMO = After watching 2 winning candles in a row
- Fear = After losing 3% on a clean setup
- Tilt = When price hits TP1 and reverses before full TP

  This maps your *emotional landmines*—so you can defuse them before stepping on them.

2. Rate of Clicks = Risk Alert System ***(Gray Hat Quant Behavior Trick)***

Install a **mouse or hotkey tracker** (e.g., AutoHotKey logs, StreamDeck stats) to **measure clicks per hour**.
Spike in clicks = emotional overdrive.
Trigger an alert:

> "Your click rate just jumped 200%. Are you trading or reacting?"
>
> This passive feedback loop is used by some algo traders to avoid human override under stress.

3. Missed Trade Reframing Ritual

Every time you miss a move, **journal it like a win** using this format:

- Setup: ✔
- Entry criteria: ✖
- Plan followed: ✅
- Emotional override: ✖
- Reward yourself for *not chasing*. This retrains your brain to **release the idea of "missing out"** and reinforces identity as a rules-based trader.

4. Biological Reset Protocol

When in tilt, don't just "take a break." **Reset your biochemistry.**
Quick stack:

- Cold water on face (vagus nerve)
- 30-second wall sit (fight/flight disruptor)

- Slow nasal breathing (3 mins)

  This snapback combo comes from **performance physiology** used by military snipers to reset under pressure.

5. "Trap Setup" Trading Rewind Drill

Save screenshots of every FOMO trade you took that failed. Label them **TRAP SETUPS**.

Once a week, review them in rapid slideshow mode—5 seconds each.

Why? It builds subconscious *visual pattern disgust* for chasing. You start **feeling allergic to impulsive entries**.

6. The "Daily Two-Sentence Limit" Rule *(For Emotional Narratives)*

When logging emotional trades, only allow **two sentences max** to describe the feeling.

- Sentence 1: "What I felt."
- Sentence 2: "What I did about it."
- Prevents drama journaling. Forces responsibility. Traders who adopt this stop spiraling into self-loathing loops.

7. Exit Ritual Compression

Most traders tilt *after* a loss, not during it. Create a **5-minute ritual immediately after a red trade**:

- Breathe
- Mark the reason
- Walk away for 60 seconds

- This becomes **muscle memory for emotional decompression.** Traders who hardwire this see a dramatic drop in revenge trades.

8. "Silent Session Stack" Mastery Mode

Once a week, schedule a full session where **you are not allowed to enter any trades**.

Do:

- Mark setups
- Log observations
- Grade your impulse level every 30 minutes

  This rewires your nervous system to *normalize non-participation*—the most undertrained skill in trading.

9. Impulse Delay Training

Use a **physical delay anchor** before every trade:

- Must stand up
- Clap your hands 3x
- Breathe, then enter
- This is *embodied pattern interruption.* Elite athletes use similar rituals to **switch brain states before key decisions.**

10. The "Stoic Trading Room" Protocol

Install Stoic philosophy principles into your pre-trade environment:

- Memento Mori reminder: "This trade is not your identity."
- Amor Fati card: "Embrace what the market gives."

- Premeditatio Malorum: Visualize your stop being hit—and being calm about it.

  Some funded traders have physical Stoic quotes taped to their monitors. This reframes every trade through the lens of resilience, not perfection.

Final Word

Emotion doesn't vanish with experience. It **evolves.** These tactics are how the best traders train to feel everything—**and still execute clean.**

You don't defeat emotion. You outlast it with process.

In the next chapter, we're going to tackle the biggest myth in trading: that discipline is about willpower.

It's not.

It's about design.

We'll break down why motivation always fails, how to build habits that hold up under pressure, and the systems that make self-control automatic—even on your worst days.

CHAPTER 5

The Iron Mind Protocol

Mental toughness training
for high-stakes execution

Section 1: The Endurance Trading Model

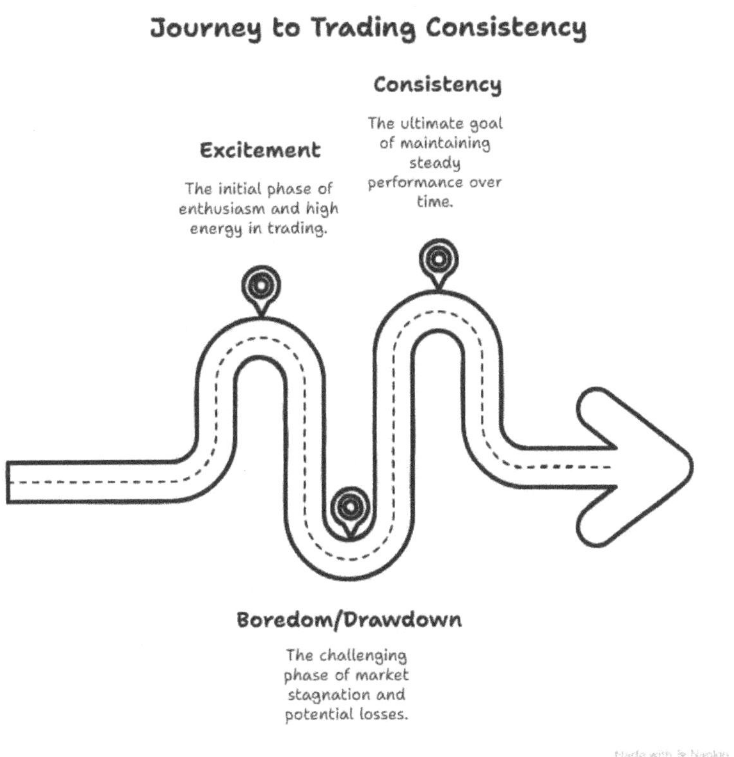

When most traders think about improving, they think in terms of skill: better entries, cleaner exits, sharper analysis. But what separates professionals from the rest isn't just skill—it's **endurance**.

Endurance isn't how long you can stare at charts. It's how consistently you can perform your process under pressure, boredom, fatigue, and loss. The market doesn't just test your edge—it tests your ability to stay *yourself* over hundreds of trades, dozens of sessions, and long streaks of emotional turbulence.

Great trading isn't about intensity. It's about repetition. Calm, focused, sometimes boring repetition. And that's exactly what this section is about: building a mind that doesn't crack over time.

Trading Like an Ultra-Marathoner

Ultra-marathoners don't train to be fast. They train to *survive* the miles. It's about pacing, energy management, and the mental toughness to keep going when the pain starts whispering, "Stop."

That's exactly what professional trading demands.

It's not about catching one big move. It's about showing up every day with the same level of discipline after a win, a loss, or a string of nothing. Ultra-endurance athletes train their bodies to keep moving even when they're depleted. As traders, we train our minds to keep executing when we're distracted, frustrated, or unsure.

That means no emotional sprinting. No jumping between strategies. No crashing after a good week. It means slow, steady, strategic behavior—every day, for months and years.

Simulated Fatigue Drills

Most traders collapse not because they don't know what to do, but because they stop doing it when their mental energy dips. The moment stress hits or boredom kicks in, their system breaks down.

Simulated fatigue drills are your answer.

Start by journaling after a bad trade. Not when it's convenient—when it's uncomfortable. Do your routine *after* you're emotionally drained. Take a pre-planned setup *after* a losing streak. These are reps under fatigue.

If you only train when you feel good, you'll only perform when you feel good. And the market rarely waits for your emotions to catch up.

By practicing execution when your state is compromised, you build the exact toughness you'll need when pressure is real.

Mental Reps > Market Setups

Most traders think more chart time equals growth. But watching the market isn't the same as *training* your mind.

Mental reps are the new edge.

Pre-session visualization. Emotional rehearsals. Reading your trading plan out loud. Journaling your state before each trade. Reviewing your worst trades without flinching.

These things don't look cool. They don't go viral. But they condition your mind to act from structure instead of emotion. They build identity-based consistency.

Every time you rehearse how you want to behave, you're reinforcing the version of yourself who actually trades that way.

Most of your underperformance isn't from lack of skill—it's from layering too much thought over something simple. You hesitate, dissect, analyze, recheck... and by then, the trade's gone or worse: you force it late. Repetition builds flow. Overthinking kills it. Clarity comes from reps, not reconsideration.

100 Trade Discipline Test

You want a real metric of progress?

Track your next 100 trades. Not the PnL. Not the win rate. Just one question: *Did I follow my rules, yes or no?*

That's it.

Because most traders fail not from strategy, but from **leaks in execution**. A shortcut here. A forced trade there. A broken rule once a day, every day. And suddenly their edge is meaningless.

The 100 Trade Discipline Test is brutal—but it's honest. It strips away the excuses. You either followed your plan or you didn't.

And when you start stacking 100 clean trades in a row, the results take care of themselves.

From Mental Weakness to Fortitude

Mental toughness isn't about being emotionless. It's about making the same high-quality decisions **regardless** of how you feel.

You become mentally tough by **not negotiating** with your process.

You follow your rules after a huge win. You stick to your size after a painful loss. You journal on red days. You prep even when you're tired.

That's how weakness turns into fortitude—not in one breakthrough moment, but in hundreds of small, uncomfortable decisions that say: *I trade from discipline, not from mood.*

You don't need more hype. You need more reps. You need to prove to yourself that you can show up, over and over, and act like a professional—even when it's hard.

That's endurance. That's identity. That's how iron minds are built.

Section 2: Spartan Training for Traders

To trade like a pro, you don't need motivation. You need **mental armor**—built through repetition, discipline, and doing hard things when no one is watching. That's what Spartan training is about.

In ancient Sparta, warriors weren't trained for comfort. They were trained to operate under pressure, through pain, and with complete emotional control. The same philosophy applies to trading. If you can execute when your emotions are calm, that's good. But if you can execute when your emotions are loud, chaotic, and screaming for relief—that's elite.

Let me give you a taste of what Spartan mindset feels like. I once ran the Dolomiti Extreme Trail—55 kilometers across the Italian Alps, with 3,720 meters of elevation gain. It took me over 13 hours. Every uphill climb felt like a battle. Every descent shredded my legs. The altitude stole my breath. The trail tested my will. By hour 10, everything hurt—my muscles, my joints, even my motivation. But I kept going. Step by painful step. Not because I felt strong, but because I refused to quit. That's the essence of Spartan training. The kind of mental toughness that pushes you forward when everything inside you begs to stop.

This section is your trader gym. Not for strategy. For structure. For grit. For the mental toughness that separates the consistently funded from the consistently frustrated.

Pain Training Systems

Comfort is the enemy of growth. In trading, emotional pain is part of the territory—losses, missed opportunities, boredom, self-doubt. You can't avoid it, but you can train for it.

Pain training doesn't mean seeking failure. It means deliberately choosing discomfort in controlled ways to build emotional resilience. Cold showers. Early wake-ups. Physical workouts. Difficult journaling sessions after losses.

These aren't rituals for "toughness points." They train your nervous system to remain calm under pressure. They teach your brain that discomfort is survivable—and even productive.

Every time you put yourself in a challenging situation and stay composed, you're building the exact inner strength that will keep you disciplined on red days, slow days, and days where everything in you wants to quit.

The Limit Order Discipline Challenge

This drill is simple in design, brutal in practice. Place a valid limit order based on your system. Then walk away. Don't watch it. Don't check price. Don't hover.

If it triggers, great. If not, that's fine too.

The point isn't the outcome. The point is to *detach from outcome addiction*. This challenge rewires the brain to let go of the need for control and instant gratification—two of the biggest psychological traps in trading.

It also builds trust in your system. You stop trying to "babysit" the trade. You stop reacting to every tick. You let the market come to you, instead of chasing after it.

This is where detachment is forged—not by thinking about it, but by acting like the trader who already has it.

The Journal Before Action Rule

Before you enter a trade, stop. Open your journal. Write one sentence:

> "Here's how I'm feeling right now."

That's it. No overthinking. No analysis. Just a pause to observe your emotional state.

This small habit creates a critical interruption in the impulse loop. It gives your rational brain time to activate before your emotional brain clicks the button. It doesn't take long—but it does save you from dozens of emotional trades over time.

More importantly, it teaches you to respect your **internal environment**, not just your external analysis. Because your edge doesn't live in your chart. It lives in your ability to make the same decision under different emotional conditions.

Emotional Tolerance Benchmarks

You don't improve what you don't measure. Most traders track profit, loss, win rate. But few track their emotional strength—and that's the real edge.

Start rating yourself weekly on the following:

- How well did I handle loss?
- How patient was I waiting for setups?
- How often did I trade from emotion?

Use a 1–10 scale. Log it. Watch it.

Over time, this becomes a powerful feedback loop. You'll start seeing emotional progress the same way you track PnL. And when you see that growth, your confidence becomes *behavior-based,* not results-based.

That's the confidence that lasts.

Cold Execution Practice

Every trader has that setup that *feels wrong* in the moment—but checks all the boxes.

Cold execution is about pulling the trigger anyway.

You're not trusting your feelings. You're trusting your framework. You're proving to yourself: "I follow my system, not my state."

Cold execution is uncomfortable—but it's the ultimate sign of trader maturity. When you can place a trade that meets your rules, even while your brain whispers, "Don't do it," you've reached a level of control most never touch.

You're not just trading. You're performing.

And that performance doesn't come from hype. It comes from systems like these. Repeated. Honored. Owned.

That's how Spartan traders are made.

Section 3: Psychological Rewiring Techniques

Discipline isn't just a habit. It's a **neurological pattern**. If you've spent years reacting emotionally to discomfort—chasing wins, avoiding losses, tilting on red days—your brain has wired those patterns in. That's the bad news.

The good news? You can rewire it. With the right techniques, you can teach your nervous system to stay calm, your focus to stay clear, and your actions to stay aligned—even when your emotions don't.

This section isn't about motivation. It's about **mechanics**. Rituals that change how your brain responds to stress, risk, and uncertainty. Because trading doesn't just test your strategy—it tests your internal wiring.

Loss Acceptance Drills

Most traders treat losses like emotional events. Something to "get over." But losses aren't mistakes—they're part of the business.

If you can't emotionally accept losses, you'll always trade from a place of fear or denial. That creates hesitation, overcorrection, or revenge trading.

Loss acceptance drills reframe the experience.

Start simple: after every loss, write this line in your journal—out loud if possible:

> "This was expected. This is part of my edge. I executed clean."

Even if it stings, say it.

This isn't toxic positivity. It's identity reinforcement. You're teaching your mind: "Losses don't mean I failed. They mean I played the game like a pro."

The more you reinforce that message, the more natural it becomes. Over time, your nervous system stops flinching at red trades—and starts focusing on *execution quality*.

Dopamine Delay Framework

Most traders are addicted to **checking**.

You enter a trade and immediately start watching it tick. Every pip becomes a dopamine hit or cortisol spike. This creates a reward loop that wires your brain to seek *stimulus*, not strategy.

The solution? Break the loop.

Use the Dopamine Delay Framework. After entering a trade, set a timer—10, 15, or 30 minutes. During that time, you're not allowed to check the trade. You step away. You breathe. You do literally anything else.

Why? Because it forces you to detach. It retrains your brain to stop obsessing over results and start trusting your process.

You're delaying the hit—and in doing so, you're building long-term discipline.

Reversal Resistance Protocol

Here's what breaks most traders: they get stopped out, and immediately flip bias. They try to "catch the reversal." They let the market bully them into reactive behavior.

That's not strategy. That's emotional whiplash.

Enter the Reversal Resistance Protocol: no new trades in the same pair or direction for 30–60 minutes after a stop-out.

This simple buffer protects you from impulsive revenge setups. It gives your mind space to recalibrate. It makes sure that your next decision is driven by *analysis*, not by emotional compensation.

You're building **friction** into your process—and that friction is what saves your capital when your ego wants payback.

The Delay & Detach Exercise

Before any trade, pause for 60 seconds.

Close your eyes. Take a deep breath. Ask yourself:

> "Is this a setup—or a feeling?"

This single moment of silence can prevent hours of emotional damage. Because it moves you from reaction to reflection. From urgency to awareness.

The Delay & Detach Exercise isn't about wasting time. It's about buying **clarity**. That 60 seconds is where you decide who's going to enter this trade: the disciplined operator, or the emotionally hijacked version of you.

Pick your trader.

Stress Inoculation Through Exposure

You want to trade better under pressure? Stop avoiding it. Start training for it.

Stress inoculation is exactly what it sounds like: small, controlled doses of pressure to build emotional immunity.

How?

- Trade live on micro size—even when you're nervous.
- Take a planned setup after a losing streak.
- Simulate a losing day and walk through your recovery process.
- Record yourself during a trade and review your state.

You're not trying to avoid stress. You're trying to **normalize it**. Because once your nervous system learns that stress doesn't mean danger, it stops hijacking your behavior.

And that's the edge.

Traders who train their brains to stay calm in chaos don't flinch. They don't fumble. They don't fall apart.

They execute.

Section 4: Identity Anchoring

Most traders are chasing results, but the ones who last are chasing something deeper—**identity alignment**. Because when your identity and your behavior are in sync, discipline becomes automatic.

You stop trying to "remember" your rules. You stop negotiating with bad habits. You stop needing to psych yourself up before every session. Why? Because you're acting in alignment with who you believe you are.

That's identity anchoring—shifting your focus from *what you're doing* to *who you're becoming*. You stop asking "Did I make money?" and start asking, "Did I act like a funded trader today?"

The tools in this section help you lock that identity in place, so discipline becomes less of a struggle and more of a default setting.

The Future-Funded Self Exercise

This is one of the most powerful anchoring drills you can do. Take 5–10 minutes and write a short letter or journal entry from your future-funded self to your present-day self.

Example:

> "Here's how I trade. Here's what I do before every session. Here's how I handle losses. Here's what I never do. Here's the mindset that keeps me funded."

This version of you already exists—it just needs to be defined.

Read this before your trading sessions. Let it act like a filter. If your current behavior doesn't match what your future-funded self would do, don't do it. Simple.

You're not trading to become that version—you're trading *as if* you already are.

Self-Talk Script Rewrite

Your internal dialogue either reinforces identity—or sabotages it.

Listen to how you talk to yourself during a trade. Do you hear things like:

- "I hope this works..."
- "Please don't reverse..."
- "Let me just try this one..."

These are the scripts of uncertainty, not professionalism.

Now rewrite them:

- "I'm executing a plan I trust."
- "This is a high-quality setup. The outcome doesn't define me."
- "My role is execution. The market decides the rest."

Say them. Write them. Post them on your wall if you need to.

Because language isn't just communication—it's **conditioning**. The more you speak like a professional, the more your mind accepts that identity. And the more natural your discipline becomes.

Behavior-Based Confidence

Forget trying to build confidence from your PnL. That's the fastest way to ride an emotional rollercoaster.

Confidence built on outcomes is fragile. Confidence built on *behavior* is bulletproof.

When you follow your plan—even on a red day—you build trust. When you stay patient—even in a dry market—you build belief. When you journal after a losing streak—you build self-respect.

These are the deposits you make into your identity account.

The next time you doubt yourself, ask: *Have I been acting like the trader I want to become?*

If the answer is yes, you're already winning. If the answer is no, fix the behavior—not the outcome.

Discipline as Identity Currency

Every time you follow your rules, you're casting a vote for the type of trader you are.

And like money, those votes compound.

One clean session becomes two. One day without overtrading becomes a week. One moment of emotional control becomes a pattern.

You're not just building habits. You're building a *self-concept*.

And once discipline becomes part of your identity, you stop relying on willpower. You stop fighting against yourself. You start doing what needs to be done—not because it feels good, but because it feels **normal**.

That's when trading gets powerful.

"Trade It Like You Own It" Drill

Here's the framing shift that upgrades everything:

> "Trade every account like it's your family's savings. Like it's real. Like it matters."

Because it does.

Even if your position is $0.50 per pip, even if your size is small, act like it's a million-dollar account. Ask yourself before every trade:

- Would I still take this if it was 100K on the line?
- Would I still size this way if it affected my reputation?
- Would I still click this if this was my business capital?

This drill reframes your relationship with responsibility. It upgrades your standard. It forces you to act with precision, care, and respect.

That mindset becomes identity. And that identity builds longevity.

You're not just trading anymore. You're representing the version of yourself that earns and protects capital with intention.

Section 5: Takeaway Principle: "Discipline Isn't a Mood. It's a Muscle."

Discipline is the most misunderstood trait in trading. Most think it's about willpower—something you wake up with on good days and lose on bad ones. But that's not discipline. That's mood management.

Real discipline doesn't care how you feel. It doesn't depend on motivation, clarity, or whether the trade "feels good." Real discipline is **trained**—and more importantly, it's trained like a **muscle**.

You don't build muscle by thinking about it. You build it by **repetition under resistance.** The same is true for your trading psychology.

Discipline Isn't Emotional — It's Mechanical

Here's the first shift: stop treating discipline as an emotional event. It's not something that hits you in a wave of inspiration. It's not tied to confidence or clarity. It's a **mechanical pattern**.

You wake up. You follow your pre-market routine. You journal your state. You wait for your setup. You enter by rules. You size correctly. You log the trade.

That process doesn't care if you're tired. Or excited. Or afraid. It's mechanical. The moment you start acting from routine instead of feeling, discipline stops being effort—it becomes **automation**.

That's the goal.

Every Act of Discipline is a Rep

When you pass on a subpar setup, that's a rep.
When you follow your max daily loss rule, that's a rep.

When you journal after a loss you didn't want to look at, that's a rep. When you follow your limit order instead of chasing price, that's a rep.

And just like reps in the gym, each one builds strength. At first, it's hard. Unnatural. It feels like you're fighting yourself. But the more reps you do, the stronger your identity becomes. Until one day, following your rules is just *how you operate.*

You don't even think about it. It's built in.

Traders Don't Rise to Their Strategy. They Fall to Their Identity.

It doesn't matter how sharp your setup is if you can't follow it when emotions spike. You don't rise to the quality of your analysis—you fall to the **strength of your identity under pressure.**

And your identity? It's built by behavior.

This is why some traders do great in backtesting and fail in live execution. They have intellectual clarity but no **emotional endurance**. They haven't trained the muscle of discipline under fire.

If you want to hold form when the market punches you in the face, you need more than a strategy. You need a structure you can rely on—because it's been **repped into muscle memory.**

Discipline Can't Be Borrowed. It Must Be Built.

You can learn strategies from other traders. You can copy risk models, journaling templates, even routines.

But you can't **borrow discipline**.

It has to be earned through experience. Through sweat. Through tiny, unsexy decisions repeated without applause.

It's built at 5am when you don't want to prep.
It's built after three losses when you want to force the next trade.
It's built in the moment you pause, breathe, and still follow the plan.

That's how professionals are made.

You're Not Training to Trade Perfectly. You're Training to Trade Consistently.

Perfection is an illusion. Consistency is the real edge.

And consistency comes from muscle—repeated behaviors that hold their shape under stress. Not because you feel great, but because you've trained to act aligned *regardless* of how you feel.

Discipline isn't supposed to be exciting. It's supposed to be stable. Grounded. Reliable.

You build it one rep at a time.

Final Thought:

Every time you trade with discipline, you vote for the future version of yourself you say you want to become. You cast a ballot that says, "I am this type of trader."

That's how identity forms. That's how confidence grows. That's how accounts scale.

Discipline isn't a mood. It's a muscle. Build it like your career depends on it—because it does.

10 Underground Hacks to Build an Unbreakable Trader Mindset

These tactics weren't invented by me—they were collected. I've found them in trading books, deep-dive tutorials, YouTube videos, and the occasional private group or paid course. Some are well-hidden, others are just underused—but together, they form a playbook of practical, powerful ways to upgrade how you trade.

1. The 10-Second Ego Lock

Before every trade, whisper this aloud:

> **"This trade is not about me."**
> It disarms the identity attachment. Traders at top firms use verbal pattern interrupters to sever ego ties before risk is deployed. Try it for 30 days. You'll stop trading like your self-worth is on the line.

2. Cold Pre-Session Priming *(Physio-Neuro Hack)*

Splash ice water on your face, or do 30 seconds of cold exposure before charts. This triggers the mammalian dive reflex, reducing heart rate and stress hormones.

Used in **combat stress inoculation programs** and now quietly in high-performance trading circles.

> You're hacking your vagus nerve = instant calm.

3. The Red Candle Ritual

Whenever you get stopped out, immediately:

- Sit still for 15 seconds.
- Take a breath.
- Write one sentence in your journal:

  "That was a clean loss. I execute. I do not react."
  This rewires the stop-loss event from emotional rupture → identity reinforcement.

4. Discipline Budgeting

Track **how many "discipline points" you have per session**. Just like energy, discipline depletes.
Create a daily cap (e.g., 5 decision points). Log each:

- One for waiting
- One for passing a FOMO setup
- One for journaling after a red trade

  Once you hit your "budget," end the session. Keeps you from burnout + overtrading spirals.

5. Sensory Suppression Drill ***(Gray Hat Sensory Hack)***

Trade one session with your monitor's brightness cut in half and all audio distractions removed. No music. No alerts.
Why? It **increases mental load** slightly, simulating decision fatigue. Doing this once a week boosts mental resilience during live chaos.

> Prop firms simulate distraction environments to test execution clarity. This mimics that.

6. The Spartan Day Protocol

Once a week, run a full trading session under "Spartan Rules":

- No coffee
- No music
- No alerts
- Execute trades from memory
- This is **trading under deprivation**, not performance. Why? To train pure process recall and emotional control when comfort is stripped. It's hellish. It's priceless.

7. Auto-Recap Habit Stack

Use a tool (e.g., Otter, Loom) to record a **verbal recap at end of day.** Not your trades—your discipline. Ask:

- "Where did I hesitate?"
- "Where did I break form?"
- "What emotion showed up strongest today?"
- This becomes a *mirror of your mental reps*. Most traders never watch their own mindset in motion. Do this, and you separate from 95% of the herd.

8. The Micro-Penalty Stack *(Discipline Conditioning)*

Set a tiny "punishment" for breaking process:

- Miss a journal entry? 25 pushups.
- Revenge click? Cold shower.
- Overtrade? Donate $10 to a cause you dislike.
- This isn't masochistic—it's **habit loop reinforcement.** You're associating emotional decisions with consequences, not comfort.

9. The Invisible Win Tracker

Track **zero PnL for 30 days.** Instead, log:

- Number of clean trades executed
- Number of setups passed on discipline
- Number of emotional overrides prevented

At the end? You'll have **behavior-based performance metrics**—which are far more predictive of success than a single streak.

10. Pre-Funded Identity Contracts

Before you scale size, write a "trader contract" with these questions:

- How do I behave during drawdowns?
- What emotions sabotage me most?
- What version of me is not allowed to click this size?

Then **sign it**, print it, and post it above your screen.

> This creates *pre-committed behavioral boundaries*—a secret technique used by private fund managers to filter out FOMO-prone traders.

Final Word

You don't build an iron mind by thinking positive. You **build it with reps under resistance**. Every act of delayed gratification, of rule-following, of emotional detachment—that's a curl for your mental muscle.

> **Discipline is not a vibe. It's a reflex you train in silence until it roars under pressure.**

CHAPTER 6

Mindset Misfires – The 10 Psychological Mistakes Killing Your Account

A forensic breakdown of what separates winners from blowups

This chapter is a mirror. Ten of them, actually.

Each one reflects a subtle mindset flaw that slowly eats away at your account, your consistency, and your confidence. These aren't surface-level problems. They're identity leaks—psychological habits that feel small in the moment but compound into chaos over time.

We're not here to shame. We're here to diagnose, reframe, and fix. For each misfire, you'll get a clear metaphor, a practical drill, and a journal prompt to rewire it.

Let's get into it.

1. Validation Seeking

Diagnosis:

Validation seeking is one of the most deceptive psychological traps in trading. On the surface, it looks like enthusiasm—you're proud of your trades, excited to share your wins, posting your PnL screenshots, getting engagement on Discord or Telegram. But underneath that? You're not trading for growth. You're trading to be seen.

You start trading for the highlight reel instead of the long game. You want applause, not accuracy. And over time, that need to impress starts infecting your decisions. You take riskier trades to chase a story. You overtrade because it's been a slow week and you want something to share. You avoid logging red days because they don't fit the image.

Validation-seeking shifts your focus from internal alignment to external attention. And when that happens, you're no longer a trader. You're a performer.

Metaphor:

It's like going to the gym just to take mirror selfies. You're not lifting for strength—you're lifting for likes. You're more concerned with *looking* like a professional than *becoming* one. And just like muscles built for show don't last under real weight, trades taken for clout don't hold up under real pressure.

Fix:

Cut off all sources of external validation for 30 days. No trade sharing. No screenshots. No talking about gains. Trade silently. The goal is to rebuild your relationship with the craft—not the crowd.

Drill:

Silent Sessions. Block out feedback. No social media, no chat rooms, no performance talk. Just you, your chart, your system, and your journal. End each session with a reflection on your *process*, not your result.

Journal Prompt:

"If no one saw this trade, would I still take it?"
Write this before every entry for the next 7 days. If the answer isn't a clear yes, don't click. Train yourself to trade for consistency, not recognition.

2. Urgency Addiction

Diagnosis:

Urgency addiction is that compulsive need to *click now*. You see price moving. Your setup looks like it's about to trigger. Your heart rate rises. You skip the final confirmation. Your finger's already on the mouse. You're in.

And then price reverses.

The worst part? You *knew* it wasn't ready. But you didn't want to wait. Because waiting feels like losing. It feels like letting something slip through your fingers. That discomfort—the gap between seeing the setup and taking the setup—becomes unbearable. So you jump early just to make it go away.

That's not a trading decision. That's emotional escape.

Over time, this habit destroys your edge. You take half-baked entries, get stopped out, and then watch the trade play out exactly as planned—without you. Not because your strategy failed, but because you refused to slow down.

Metaphor:

It's like walking a dog that pulls on the leash the moment it sees something interesting. Except the dog is your brain. And the leash? That's supposed to be your trading plan. You're not guiding your actions—your impulses are dragging *you* across the chart.

Fix:

You need to create friction. Add a deliberate pause between analysis and action. The space between seeing the trade and clicking it is where clarity lives. And more importantly—where regret gets prevented.

Drill:

The 60-Second Stall. Before every trade, start a timer. Breathe. Review your rules. Confirm your entry criteria. Ask yourself: "What's the rush?" This one-minute pause is your mental reset button.

Journal Prompt:

"What am I afraid of missing right now?"
Write this the moment you feel urgency. You'll often discover it's not the trade you're scared of missing—it's the *feeling* of certainty. Trade your plan, not your need for speed.

3. Strategy Hopping

Diagnosis:

Strategy hopping is one of the most common and costly trader habits. It happens when you abandon your system—not because it's invalid, but because it didn't give you what you wanted fast enough. One red week? Time to try a new indicator. Two missed entries? Time to watch another YouTube backtest. You're constantly scanning for a better edge, a faster signal, or a "more accurate" setup.

The truth? You're not testing strategies—you're avoiding discomfort. The discomfort of waiting. Of losing. Of uncertainty. And instead of building depth with one method, you stay shallow with many.

Strategy hopping kills confidence. You never stay long enough with one system to build trust. You never develop true intuition, because you don't allow pattern repetition to take hold. You keep restarting the journey at step one.

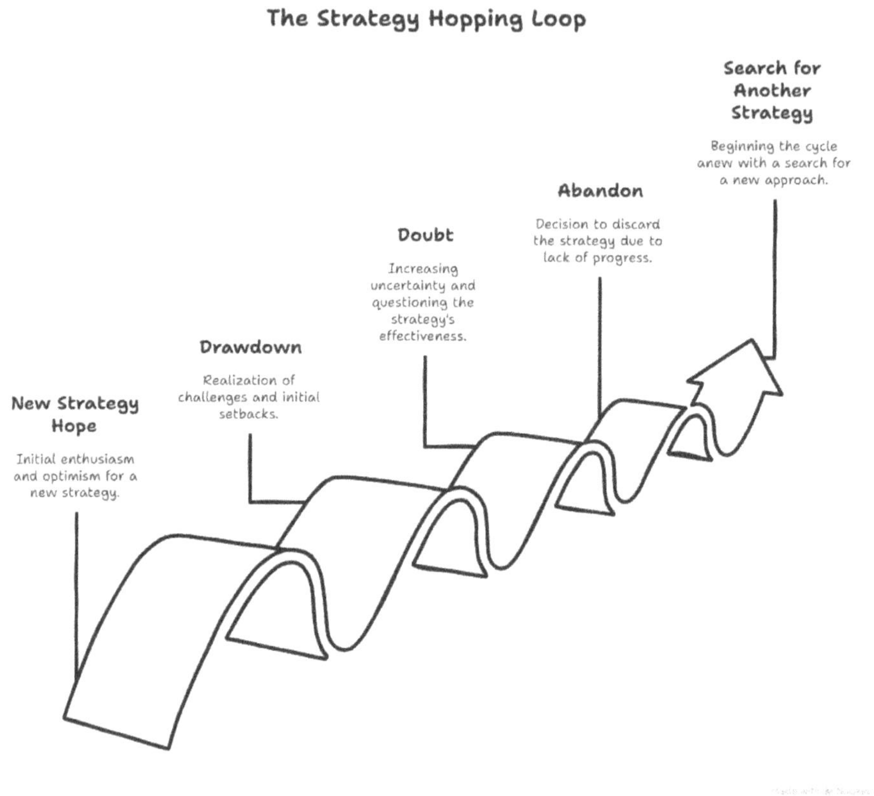

Metaphor:

It's like planting a seed and digging it up every few days to check if it's growing. You never give it time to take root. So the soil gets disturbed. The growth gets disrupted. And you convince yourself the seed is broken, when really, *your impatience is the problem.*

Fix:

Pick one framework. One setup type. One clear entry model. Commit to 100 trades using it. That's the real test—not "Does it work in five trades?" but "Can I stay consistent long enough to find out?"

Drill:

The 100 Trade Commitment Tracker. Create a spreadsheet or physical chart. For each trade, log only two things:

1. Did I follow my rules?
2. Did I break discipline?

Forget PnL. Focus on process.

Before you earn the right to change your system, you must track it. No system should be evaluated without 100 solid trades behind it. Emotion makes you tweak too soon. Data keeps you honest. Your system might not be broken—you might just be jumping ship before the ship even leaves the dock.

But that doesn't mean blind faith. There are objective metrics every strategy must be judged by. Max Drawdown. Win Rate. Max Consecutive Losses. Return-to-Drawdown Ratio. If those numbers drift outside your acceptable performance zone, that's when you re-optimize or pause the system. But if your metrics are holding steady—even through a losing streak—your job is to stay the course. You don't ditch a good engine just because the weather changes. You monitor it, trust it, and stay consistent. Let your stats speak louder than your mood.

Journal Prompt:

"What am I hoping to avoid by switching?"
Often, the answer is deeper than trading: failure, boredom, self-doubt. Write it out. Bring it to the surface. Because once you know what you're really running from, you can finally stop. And grow.

4. Perfectionism Paralysis

Diagnosis:

Perfectionism paralysis is subtle but deadly. It hides behind the mask of high standards. It convinces you that you're being "disciplined" or "selective," when really—you're just scared to be wrong.

You hesitate on setups that are 80% clean, waiting for them to become 100% ideal. But in trading, 100% never comes. There's always a candle that's a little too big, a wick that doesn't line up, or an RSI reading you're unsure about. And while you're over-analyzing, the market moves without you.

The result? Missed trades. Constant frustration. And a warped sense of success that's based on *certainty*, not *execution*.

The deeper truth? Perfectionism isn't about wanting quality. It's about avoiding discomfort—specifically, the discomfort of taking a valid trade and still losing. If your standard is "only enter when it's perfect," then you never have to feel the sting of being wrong *while doing everything right.*

But that sting is part of being a trader. Avoiding it delays your growth.

Metaphor:

It's like sitting in front of a blank page, trying to write the perfect sentence before you write anything at all. You're so afraid of writing something flawed, you never even start the paragraph. Meanwhile, others are writing, editing, improving—and publishing.

Fix:

Redefine success. It's not about getting the cleanest setup. It's about taking valid trades with clean process—even when they feel slightly uncomfortable. That's where real growth happens.

Drill:

B+ Trade Challenge. For the next 10 sessions, take trades that meet your system rules—even if they're not "perfect." Full process. Full journal. Then review how many of those "imperfect" trades still played out.

Journal Prompt:

"What does perfect protect me from?"
Get honest. Usually, the answer is: judgment, fear, exposure. But the more you avoid that fear, the more you avoid the trades that grow you.

Let me tell you a story that illustrates how perfectionism can trap us—and how pivoting can be a trader's greatest strength.

I don't celebrate birthdays like most people. For my 40th, I flew to Italy, determined to run around Lake Garda—25 km a day for eight days, with serious elevation through the mountains. I'd dreamed of this trip for years—Lake Garda is one of the most stunning places on Earth. It was supposed to be my ultra marathon birthday celebration.

Then it happened: on Day 3—my actual birthday—I injured my left foot. Limping the final 15 km into Limone Sul Garda that evening, I realized the plan was dead. I celebrated with a quiet soak in a hot tub, not the triumphant finish I'd imagined. Perfectionism would have had me give up the whole trip. But I didn't.

I adapted. I rented a bike and set a new goal: circumnavigate Lake Garda in three days. Starting the next morning, I pedaled hard—climbing steep switchbacks, coasting through olive groves, and stopping in hidden villages to photograph sunsets over the water. Over 180 km and epic scenery later, I completed the journey. No pain-free runs, but a profound win.

Couple of years later, sharing the story with my son in Limone pulled everything into focus. He was fascinated—not by my running failure, but by my choice to adapt and triumph anyway. That's the shift I want every trader to feel.

Markets don't wait for perfect setups. Breaks happen. Signals fail. Conditions change. Perfectionism makes you see failure as failure—instead of an invitation to pivot. The Lake Garda pivot taught me this: when your original plan dies, you don't fold. You replan. You adapt. You stay in the game.

Whether it's trading or training, success isn't about flawless execution. It's about resilience and flexibility. The ability to adjust your path, not abandon your mission. That's the kind of trader who doesn't just recover from a loss—but thrives beyond it.

5. Rule Rebellion

Diagnosis:

Rule rebellion is when you become your own enemy—not by ignorance, but by choice. You know your rules. You wrote them. You've repeated them to yourself countless times. And yet, in the heat of the moment—right after a big win or a frustrating loss—you break them.

Maybe you increase size because you're "feeling it." Maybe you take one more trade even though you've hit your daily max. Maybe you enter without confirmation because you *just know* it's going to go.

In these moments, you're not trading your system. You're trading your ego. And the market is ruthless with ego.

The dangerous part about rule rebellion is that sometimes it works. You break your rules… and win. And now your brain has a new idea: *Maybe the rules are optional.* But that's the beginning of a slow burn. Because if you only follow your process when it's easy or convenient, you don't actually have a process. You have suggestions—and suggestions collapse under pressure.

Metaphor:

It's like creating a clean eating plan on Monday and promising yourself you'll stick to it. Then Tuesday comes, and after one stressful meeting, you're eating cake in the break room. You didn't forget the plan—you overrode it with emotion.

Fix:

Create consequences. If you break a rule, there must be a cost. Not to punish yourself—but to add weight to the decision. A tangible consequence keeps you accountable when your emotions try to override your logic.

Drill:

The Rule Violation Tax Jar. Pick your currency—$10, 20 push-ups, 15 minutes of chart review. Every time you break a rule, pay the tax. Make rule-breaking uncomfortable, not casual.

Journal Prompt:

"What part of me thinks the rules don't apply right now?"
Dig deep. There's usually a voice whispering, *"This time is different,"* or *"I can get away with it."* Shine light on that voice. Then trade from structure—not excuses.

6. Overleveraging

Diagnosis:

Overleveraging is a silent killer. It disguises itself as ambition, confidence, or urgency—but underneath, it's almost always driven by fear or desperation. You size up to "catch up" after a losing streak. You add lots to a position because you want to hit your profit target faster. Or maybe you're riding high after a win and think, *"I'm on fire today."*

In every case, the logic is the same: *More size equals faster results.*

But here's the truth—when you overleverage, you're not increasing your edge. You're just multiplying the emotional load. Every pip feels like a gut punch. Every tick in the wrong direction turns into a panic trigger. Your nervous system goes into fight-or-flight mode, and suddenly your clear process is gone.

You're no longer trading. You're **surviving**.

And ironically, the very thing you were trying to accelerate—your growth—is now at risk of total derailment.

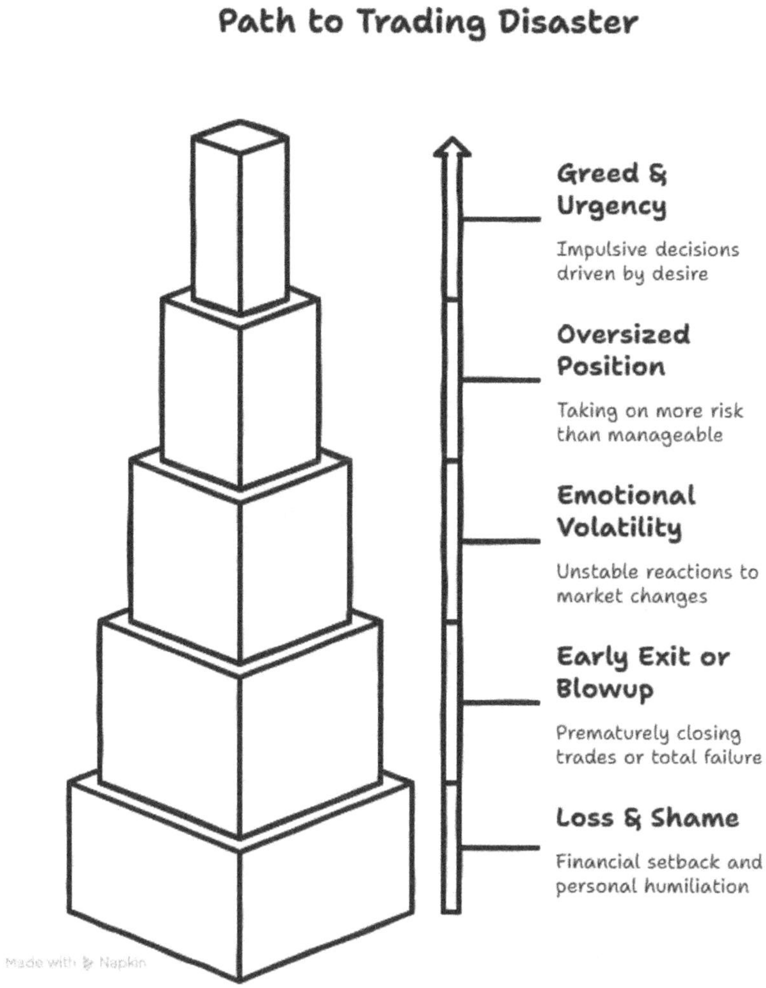

Metaphor:

It's like trying to fix a cracked windshield by hitting the gas harder. You see the damage, you feel the urgency, so you push forward with more force. But pressure doesn't fix cracks. It **shatters** what's already fragile.

Fix:

Decide your max risk per trade—percentage or dollar-based—and write it down. Then commit to following it for 30 consecutive trades. No exceptions. You don't earn the right to scale until your discipline proves it can handle size.

Drill:

Micro-size for 10 trades. Trade so small you don't care about the outcome. Focus only on clean execution. If you can't stay process-oriented at small size, you'll fall apart at size that matters. After 10 trades, increase *only* if your behavior is consistent.

Journal Prompt:

"What belief is fueling this position size?"
Is it fear of missing out? Is it revenge? Is it a fantasy of one trade changing everything? Be honest. Because until you fix the belief, the behavior won't change.

7. Fear of Losing

Diagnosis:

The fear of losing is the most ironic trading flaw: you're afraid of something that's guaranteed. Losses are part of every legitimate system, no matter how strong. But when you associate a losing trade with personal failure, you start avoiding the very moves that make you profitable in the long run.

You hesitate on clean setups. You double-check everything. You wait for more confirmation. You skip the trade altogether. Not because it doesn't meet your rules—but because you don't want to feel the sting of being wrong.

This fear warps your edge. You start filtering trades through emotion instead of execution. And slowly, you become a perfectionist in disguise—someone who would rather "stay flat" than risk being uncomfortable.

Metaphor:

It's like a boxer who refuses to throw a punch because they don't want to get hit. They circle the ring, hands up, staying safe… but they never score. And eventually, they lose anyway—because you can't win if you don't engage.

Fix:

You must separate loss from identity. A red trade isn't a reflection of your intelligence, value, or potential. It's feedback. It's one in a long series of probabilities that, over time, define your edge. Your job isn't to avoid losing—it's to manage it with calm, structure, and repetition.

Drill:

Loss Library. Every time you take a trade that follows your plan and ends in a loss, screenshot it. Log the entry, exit, reason for entry, and your emotional state. Review this weekly—not to shame yourself, but to **normalize** the presence of red. This reconditions your nervous system to see losses as neutral.

Journal Prompt:

"If this trade loses, what story am I telling myself?"

Is it "I'm not cut out for this"? Is it "I'll never be consistent"? Call out the story. Challenge it. Because most of the fear isn't about the trade—it's about the meaning you've attached to it.

8. Emotional Trading

Diagnosis:

Emotional trading is what happens when you let your state—not your system—make the decisions. You're frustrated from a loss and take a revenge trade. You're bored and force an entry just to "feel in control." You're overly excited from a win and decide to size up without thinking.

These trades weren't planned—they were reactions. And the moment your trades become emotional reactions, your edge disappears. You start to blur the line between following your process and chasing a feeling. What used to be structured becomes impulsive. What used to be intentional becomes erratic.

Emotional trading is deceptive. It often starts small—one rushed entry, one "just this once" impulse. But over time, it erodes trust in yourself. You begin to fear your own behavior, not the market.

Metaphor:

It's like driving drunk. You might stay on the road for a while. You might even get home. But you're not really in control. You're unpredictable, dangerous, and one sharp turn from disaster. The fact that you didn't crash this time doesn't mean it was safe. It means you got lucky.

Fix:

Build the habit of self-checks. Insert micro-pauses between your thoughts and your actions. You don't need to eliminate emotion—you need to become aware of it *before* it makes decisions for you.

Drill:

Emotion Tagging. Before every trade, write down or speak out the dominant emotion you're feeling. Even just one word—"calm," "rushed," "hopeful," "annoyed." This doesn't stop the emotion, but it makes it conscious. And once it's conscious, you can choose whether or not to let it lead.

Journal Prompt:

"What emotion is currently trying to take the wheel?"
This question can stop a thousand bad trades. Because if the answer isn't "none" or "focused," it's time to pause. Let the system drive—not the surge of adrenaline, frustration, or fear.

9. Execution Avoidance

Diagnosis:

Execution avoidance is the quiet killer of trading careers. It doesn't look like recklessness—it looks like productivity. You study charts. You refine your strategy. You journal, plan, review... and then freeze when it's time to enter.

This isn't laziness. It's **over-preparation masking fear**.

You've convinced yourself that if you just tweak your system a little more, backtest one more setup, or watch one more candle, you'll feel "ready." But in reality, readiness is a lie. You're not avoiding action because you lack information—you're avoiding the emotional risk of being wrong, losing money, or confronting uncertainty.

Avoiding trades keeps you safe from short-term discomfort—but it also keeps you stuck. And you can't build confidence or experience without *execution*.

Metaphor:

It's like spending months sharpening a sword but never stepping into the arena. You polish it, admire it, adjust its grip… but you never swing it. And no matter how sharp it gets, it doesn't make you a warrior. You have to fight. That's where skill is forged.

Fix:

Create accountability that forces you to act. Execution doesn't have to mean full-size or full conviction. It just means taking *one step forward*—even small—every session.

Drill:

Daily Micro-Commitment. Every trading session, commit to placing one trade—even at minimum size. The goal is to normalize action. Don't overthink it. Follow your plan. Even if it's a demo or symbolic trade, the repetition rewires the fear loop and builds trust through action.

Journal Prompt:

"What fear is hiding behind my preparation?"

Is it fear of failure? Fear of success? Fear of judgment? Write it out. Because when you name the fear, it loses power. Execution isn't the final step—it's the *bridge* between potential and progress. Cross it daily.

10. Victim Mindset & No Journaling

Diagnosis:

The victim mindset is one of the most dangerous patterns in trading—not because it's loud, but because it's subtle. It shows up in phrases like:

- "The market was manipulated."
- "The spread was too wide."
- "News hit out of nowhere."
- "The broker screwed me."

Are these things sometimes true? Sure. But when your default is to blame *everything* but yourself, you rob yourself of the most important tool a trader has: **control**.

Pair this mindset with a lack of journaling, and you create a recipe for stagnation. No review. No reflection. No growth. You're too busy pointing fingers to see where your behavior actually played a role.

Metaphor:

It's like blaming the rain every time your roof leaks, but refusing to patch the hole. The storm isn't the problem—it's the fact that you won't take ownership of the fix.

You can't control the market. But you can control your process, your mindset, your discipline, and your decisions. That's where progress begins.

Fix:

Adopt **radical ownership**. Every outcome is yours to learn from—win or lose. Remove blame from your vocabulary. Own everything. That doesn't mean self-blame or shame—it means looking for *your piece* of the puzzle in every outcome, and taking responsibility for changing it.

Drill:

Non-Negotiable Journaling. After every session—win, loss, or no trades—set a 2-minute timer and journal:

- What went well?
- What did I miss?
- What did I feel?

Do this *every single day.* No exceptions. This builds emotional awareness and transforms your trading into a self-audit tool.

Journal Prompt:

"What did I contribute to today's outcome—good or bad?"
Write without defensiveness. Be specific. Be honest. Because the trader who owns everything becomes the trader who can change anything. That's how you shift from victim to victor.

Takeaway Principle

"You Don't Rise to the Level of Your Strategy. You Fall to the Level of Your Mindset."

This is the truth most traders don't want to hear—but absolutely need to. Everyone is obsessed with strategy: the perfect entry, the cleanest indicator, the most precise risk-reward ratio. And while strategy matters, it's not the deciding factor.

Because under pressure, you won't default to the highest level of your knowledge—you'll default to the deepest wiring of your mindset.

If your internal operating system is driven by fear, impulsiveness, perfectionism, or ego, it doesn't matter how solid your plan is. You'll sabotage it the moment stress enters the room.

Think of two traders using the exact same system. One executes it with patience, detachment, and discipline. The other jumps in early, chases losses, and tweaks the rules after every red trade. The outcome? Worlds apart—not because of the strategy, but because of the **psychology behind the screen**.

Your edge doesn't live in the chart setup. It lives in your **emotional state during execution**. It lives in your ability to wait when it's boring, to hold when it's uncomfortable, and to stay calm when it's tempting to react.

This chapter hasn't just been about mindset theory—it's been a forensic breakdown of how your internal patterns show up in your trading. And more importantly, how to rewire them.

Each misfire you correct gives you more control. Each journal prompt you answer makes you more aware. Each drill you practice builds real-time mental muscle. And over time, that stack of small inner wins becomes the foundation of something unshakable.

So stop obsessing over the next signal or secret setup.

Look inward.

The market will only reflect what's already happening inside of you.

Mindset isn't an accessory to your strategy. It's the core of your performance. Upgrade it, and everything else starts falling into place.

10 Industry-Insider Hacks to Erase the Mindset Misfires Killing Traders

These tactics come from books, tutorials, videos, and the occasional private group. I've collected what works—not what's trendy—to give you tools you can apply right now, before you're funded. Some are overlooked. A few are even a little gray hat.

1. The "No-Ego Replay" Drill

Fixes: Validation Seeking, Rule Rebellion

Record a screen session of your trades with **no mic, no edits**, just raw action. Review it 24–48 hours later **as if you're watching a stranger**.

Ask: *Would I hire this trader?*

This detachment reframes your behavior into data—removing ego from the equation. Used by internal review teams in prop firms.

2. Click Friction Hack (CFH)

Fixes: Urgency Addiction, Overleveraging

Use an AutoHotkey script or StreamDeck to **force a 3-step confirmation to enter any trade**:

- Step 1: Pre-entry checklist popup
- Step 2: Manual size confirmation
- Step 3: Click-to-proceed script
- This adds "tactical drag" to emotional speed-clicking. Think of it as putting a seatbelt on your mouse.

3. Trader Timeout Card

Fixes: Emotional Trading, Rule Rebellion

Print a physical card or sticky note:

> **"I am not allowed to trade until I complete 3 deep breaths, a rules checklist, and a 10-word intention statement."**
> Put it in front of your screen. You must touch it before any trade. This pattern interruption links physicality to discipline—used by sports psychologists with elite athletes.

4. The "Strategic Depth" Tracker

Fixes: Strategy Hopping

Build a visual dashboard (Notion, Google Sheets) with one tab per strategy. Each tab must include:

- 20+ live trade examples
- Annotated market conditions

- Win/loss + emotional notes
- This creates **commitment bias**—making you *emotionally invested* in strategy mastery. Used in institutional playbooks to prevent shallow system-switching.

5. The 80% Trade Score Drill

Fixes: Perfectionism Paralysis

Score each trade idea from 0–100 based on how closely it matches your criteria. If it hits 80%, you must enter.
This forces **acceptance of imperfection** and reinforces realistic execution. Used internally by funded traders to break "analysis paralysis."

6. Journaling Penalty Vault *(Gray Hat Conditioning)*

Fixes: No Journaling, Victim Mindset

Every day you don't journal = $5 into a "vault" (real cash). At month-end, **donate it to a cause you *disagree* with**.
Why? Pain avoidance > motivation. It builds journaling into your *identity-cost avoidance loop*.
Used by high-performance exec coaches.

7. Loss Audio Loop Rewire

Fixes: Fear of Losing, Execution Avoidance

After a clean-system loss, record a 10-second voice note:

> "This was expected. I followed my plan. This is the cost of edge."

Then replay it 3x while walking or stretching. This links **kinesthetic movement to psychological closure**—rewiring the nervous system away from trauma loops.

8. Bias Lockout Timer

Fixes: Reversal Chasing, Tilt

After a losing trade, run a 20-minute "bias lockout" timer where you're **banned from re-analyzing or re-entering** that pair.
Use a browser blocker or app timer if needed.
This mimics circuit breakers in trading firms—emotional reset via enforced downtime.

9. Trade Like You're on Trial Protocol

Fixes: Victim Mindset

Pretend you have to defend your last 3 trades in court. Document your:

- Justification
- Process alignment
- Emotional state
- This forensic model forces total ownership. Some prop coaches use this drill to **weed out excuse-prone talent** early.

10. The Mirror Trade Question

Fixes: Every Misfire

Before clicking, ask aloud:

> "Would the future me I want to become take this trade right now?"

> This invokes **time-expanded identity**—a decision filter used by elite decision-makers, from Navy SEALs to venture capitalists.

Final Word

You already mapped the psychology. These are the **surgical tools to rewire it**.

Each tactic installs *behavioral friction, identity reinforcement,* or *pattern interruption*—the three foundations of true psychological edge.

> Most traders want motivation. But pros? They build **anti-breakdown systems**—so they don't need willpower to win.

Now let's get ready for Chapter 7, where we go beyond self-control and dive into building bulletproof *process systems*—the kind that make elite behavior automatic. That's where habits meet identity, and trading becomes execution without friction.

CHAPTER 7

The Internal Edge Theory

Your true edge is invisible, emotional, and entirely self-generated.

Most traders obsess over finding "the edge." The one setup. The secret strategy. The perfect indicator. But the deeper you go into this game, the clearer it becomes: your *real* edge isn't in the charts. It's in your **behavior under pressure**.

You could hand two traders the same system—and get two completely different outcomes. Why? Because execution is emotional. Your actions are filtered through beliefs, habits, energy, and mental clarity. That internal machinery *is* the edge.

This chapter unpacks that truth—and helps you build the kind of self-generated edge that compounds quietly, but powerfully, over time.

Section 1: Myth-Busting – The Perfect Setup Fallacy

The Hidden Belief Behind Most Traders' Struggles

Even if they don't say it out loud, most traders carry a quiet belief that sounds like this: *"If I can just find the perfect strategy, everything else will fall into place."* The losses will stop. The hesitation will disappear. The fear will dissolve. The success will come automatically.

This belief is comforting—but completely false.

Because the perfect setup doesn't exist. And even if it did, it wouldn't save you from yourself. Strategy can't solve a psychological problem. A better entry won't fix a broken mindset. If your trading discipline is fragile, your process scattered, or your confidence low, no setup can carry that weight.

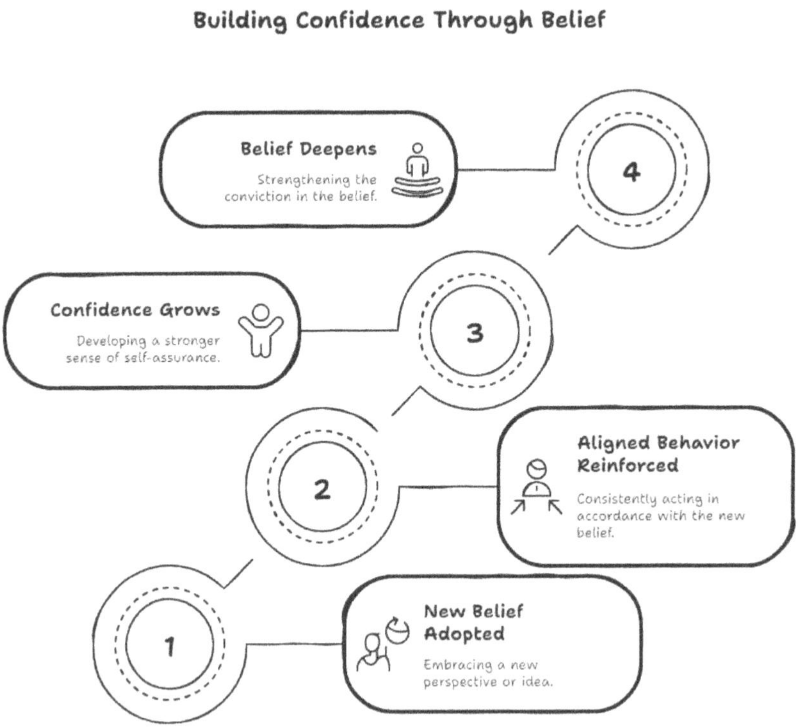

It's the Trader, Not the Tool

You can give a professional trader a basic system and they'll still be profitable. Why? Because they know how to follow rules. They know how to lose clean. They understand patience, pacing, and emotional regulation. Their edge isn't in the lines on their chart—it's in their *behavior around those lines.*

On the flip side, you can hand a brand-new trader a profitable system and they'll still find a way to blow it up. They'll enter early, size too big, hesitate on confirmation, cut winners short, or skip journaling. Not because the system doesn't work—but because *they're not ready to work it.*

The Turtle Trader Case Study

One of the most famous examples of this truth is the Turtle Traders experiment from the 1980s. Two seasoned traders, Richard Dennis and William Eckhardt, debated whether great traders were born or made. Dennis believed anyone could be taught to trade, so he set out to prove it.

He selected a group of people with zero trading experience, taught them a simple trend-following system, and gave them real capital to trade. Within a short time, many of them were generating massive profits. The secret wasn't the strategy—it was the **structure and discipline** they were taught.

The Turtle system wasn't magic. In fact, it was intentionally mechanical and emotionless. The real edge came from how consistently the traders executed it. Belief in the system gave them the confidence to act without second-guessing. That belief wasn't emotional—it was *operational.*

Setup Dependency is a Crutch

When you chase the perfect setup, you're avoiding the real work: emotional control, risk management, and process consistency. Setup dependency becomes a crutch—a way to blame the market or your system instead of owning your performance.

Traders who are setup-dependent constantly bounce between strategies. They become obsessed with filtering, tweaking, optimizing… but they never build true execution power. And execution is what actually prints money.

Strategy is a Multiplier—Not a Source

Here's the truth: a solid strategy is important. But it only multiplies what's already there. If you have self-awareness, discipline, and mental structure, a great system will elevate you. But if you're impulsive, anxious, or inconsistent, even the best system will betray you.

Think of your system as a sound system. If your mindset is clean, the signal is crisp. But if your mindset is full of noise—fear, ego, hesitation—then the output will always be distorted, no matter how good the gear is.

Belief Fuels Execution

This is where most traders miss the mark. They think they need more confirmation. More logic. More indicators. But what they really need is *belief.* Not blind faith, but earned trust in their process.

Because when you believe in your system, you stop hesitating. You stop tweaking. You stop second-guessing. You start executing.

And when you execute consistently, you give your edge room to breathe.

Stop searching for the perfect setup. Start becoming the kind of trader who can execute a simple setup *perfectly*. That's where the real edge lives. In the mirror—not the market.

Section 2: Behavior is the Real Edge

The Real Reason Traders Win Over Time

It's tempting to think that the traders who succeed are the ones with the best predictions. The ones who can forecast direction with scary accuracy. But the truth is, consistent profitability doesn't come from being *right*—it comes from being *disciplined*. The real edge isn't in calling the move. It's in how you manage yourself while the move unfolds.

Your edge is in your behavior. Period.

It's how you execute under stress. How you stay patient when the setup's not ready. How you stick to your risk model even after three losses. It's your ability to show up, every day, in alignment with your plan—not your mood.

Execution Over Excitement

Most traders chase excitement without realizing it. They love fast-moving markets. They want volatility. They live for the adrenaline of a quick win. But excitement is not a sustainable edge. In fact, it's usually the beginning of emotional leakage.

Professionals don't chase excitement. They chase **clean execution**. They treat boredom as a competitive advantage. Because they understand something retail traders often miss: *The quieter your mindset, the sharper your edge.*

If you need the market to entertain you, you're not trading—you're gaming.

Edge as Repetition Under Pressure

What makes a strategy work isn't the occasional perfect trade—it's the ability to repeat your system under *any* mental or emotional state. Tired? Still execute. Frustrated? Still execute. Bored? Still execute. Pressured? Still execute.

That's edge.

It's not just about getting it right—it's about staying right. Holding your identity, your actions, your rules *in place* while every emotion tells you to do the opposite.

Anyone can trade well in a demo account or on a good day. The edge appears when conditions are imperfect—and your behavior doesn't budge.

The 90% Rule: Mindset > Mechanics

Here's the hard truth: the difference between a trader who makes it and one who doesn't is **90% psychological**. Same charts. Same tools. Same access to information. Totally different results.

Why?

Because one of them has trained their **response**—to fear, to uncertainty, to boredom, to temptation. And the other hasn't.

The best traders don't just study markets—they study *themselves*. They realize that the only thing they truly control is their behavior. And they build systems that make disciplined behavior automatic.

From Prediction to Process

New traders want to predict. They want to be right. They spend hours looking for "confirmation" or that one extra signal that makes the trade bulletproof.

Pro traders shift from prediction to **process**. They understand that edge isn't about certainty—it's about **probability + consistency**. They aren't attached to any single outcome. They're attached to following their rules, taking high-quality setups, and executing with calm repetition.

They're not emotionally rewarded by being "right." They're rewarded by *doing what they said they would do*, regardless of the result.

This shift changes everything.

When you stop needing to be right, you stop forcing trades. You stop hesitating. You stop tweaking your system after every red trade. You become stable. Repeatable. Fundable.

Building a High-Conviction Identity

At the core of every consistently profitable trader is one thing: **identity conviction**. They believe in who they are. They believe in how they trade. They believe in their ability to take losses without breaking, to win without getting cocky, and to keep showing up even when results don't reflect effort—yet.

And belief, when backed by behavior, creates momentum that no setup can replace.

If you want to sharpen your edge, don't obsess over your entry. Obsess over your *execution habits*. That's where the real leverage is. Because the market will test you—not just on your analysis, but on your ability to stay true to your process *when it matters most*.

Section 3: Internal Metrics Dashboard

Why Most Traders Are Tracking the Wrong Things

When traders want to get serious, the first thing they usually track is their win rate. Then maybe risk-to-reward ratio, or average return per trade. These are important—but they're *surface metrics*. They show you what happened, not **why** it happened.

If you want to evolve, you need to track what's going on beneath the surface: your habits, your decision-making under pressure, your emotional regulation, and your ability to recover from setbacks. These are your **internal KPIs**—your true performance indicators.

These aren't just self-help ideas. These are measurable metrics that influence how well you can execute your edge. Let's build your internal dashboard.

Emotional Drawdown vs. Financial Drawdown

Financial drawdown is easy to see. It's on your chart. It's in your account balance. But emotional drawdown is what really causes damage. It's when you lose a trade and start questioning your system. It's when one loss triggers five more. It's when your confidence gets crushed, and you start making decisions from fear instead of structure.

Track it. Every time you have a losing streak, rate your **emotional recovery time**. How long does it take you to get back to clean execution? How long before you trust your system again? That gap matters more than the PnL.

Real confidence doesn't come from winning. It comes from not quitting after losing. Every day you survive bad trades, recover, and execute cleanly—that's a confidence deposit. Build your resilience bank, not just your profit sheet.

Mental Capital Utilization

You only have so much mental energy per day. If you use it all on over-analysis, fear, or hesitation, there's none left for high-quality execution.

Track how you spend it. How many hours of deep focus did you actually use on trading? How often did you make a decision after feeling mentally fried? The more you understand your mental energy patterns, the better you can structure your sessions for clarity—not chaos.

Confidence Recovery Rate

When you're in flow, trading is smooth. But what happens when you take a hit—mentally or financially? That recovery window is crucial.

Track how long it takes you to go from self-doubt to self-trust. Not when your next win comes, but when you start acting like a professional again. This is a leading indicator for long-term sustainability.

Ask yourself after every red day: *Am I trading with conviction today—or just trying not to lose again?*

Ritual Adherence Percentage

You've probably got a checklist. A pre-market routine. Maybe even some rules for when to walk away. But how often do you actually follow them?

Start tracking it. Literally. Write down your rituals. Then, at the end of each session, give yourself a percentage score:

- Did I do my breathwork?
- Did I journal before and after the trade?
- Did I pause before execution?

This gives you a **behavior-based scorecard**—one that builds consistency, not just performance.

Process Scorecard Over PnL

At the end of the week, don't just ask: "How much did I make?" Ask: "How well did I trade my plan?"

Rate yourself daily on the following:

- Patience
- Rule-following
- Impulse control
- Emotional awareness
- Execution quality

Use a 1–10 scale. Be honest. Then average it for the week. This internal score becomes your new scoreboard. If your process score is climbing, your equity curve will follow.

Final Word

Great traders don't just review trades—they review *themselves*. They know that if they master their internal performance, the external results will take care of themselves.

You're not a robot. You're a human trying to perform in a high-pressure, uncertain environment. So stop pretending your only edge is technical.

Build a dashboard that actually reflects who you are when it matters most. Because that's what the market is really responding to.

Section 4: Journaling Like a Scientist

Why Most Traders Journal Wrong

When traders hear "journaling," they often think of writing down thoughts and feelings in a loose, emotional way—like therapy with candles. But that's not what we're talking about here.

This isn't a diary. This is **data mining**.

Journaling, when done like a scientist, is a tool for optimization. It's how you find patterns in your behavior. It's how you identify the setups you sabotage, the emotional cycles that repeat, and the mental states that create clarity—or chaos.

Your trading journal isn't for venting. It's your personal *performance lab*.

Each trade you don't mentally close is like a browser tab left open. You think it doesn't matter—until your mind crashes. Closure isn't optional. Write it. Rate it. Close it.

Pattern Extraction from Pain

Every bad trade is a clue. Every impulsive click, skipped setup, or overleveraged move is a data point. And if you don't extract the pattern, you're doomed to repeat it.

Don't just log "why the trade went wrong." Ask deeper:

- What emotional state was I in before the trade?
- Was this trade plan-followed or emotionally driven?
- What was the self-talk just before execution?

The answers reveal the real issues—ones that no chart can show you. You're looking for emotional fingerprints. That's how you track behavior, not just results.

The "Loss Lab" Review System

Don't treat losses as something to brush off. Treat them as *experiments*. Create a section in your journal called "The Loss Lab." For each losing trade, break it down like this:

- Did I follow the rules?
- Was the setup valid?
- What did I feel going into it?
- What do I want to do differently next time?

Then, at the end of each week, review your loss lab. Look for repeating mistakes. See if certain emotional triggers or setups are responsible for the majority of errors. If 80% of your problems are caused by 20% of your behavior, this will uncover it.

Bias Tracking Logs

We all have biases: favoring longs, avoiding certain pairs, hesitating during news, distrusting breakouts. Most traders aren't even aware of theirs.

Build a bias tracking section in your journal. At the start of each session, write your directional bias for the day or week. Then, track whether that bias influenced your decisions—even when the chart said otherwise.

Were you trying to force a long bias into a bearish market? Did your conviction in one direction blind you to the cleaner opposite setup?

This kind of journaling trains *flexibility*, which is one of the most underrated psychological edges a trader can have.

Psychological Trigger Mapping

Start tracking what sets you off emotionally. For example:

- What triggers impatience?
- What leads to overtrading?
- What makes you hesitate on clean setups?

These aren't random. They're often connected to deeper mental associations—scarcity, fear of failure, need for control.

Map these out. Create a trigger-response journal:

- Trigger: Missed a trade.
- Immediate emotional response: Frustration.
- Behavior that followed: Forced a new entry to "make up for it."

Now you've got the blueprint. With awareness comes intervention. You can't control emotions—but you *can* control your response to them, once you see the pattern clearly.

Narrative Reframing in Trade Logs

The stories you tell yourself about your performance shape your identity. "I always screw this up" becomes a belief. "I can't trust myself after a loss" becomes a mental rule.

Reframe your narrative in your logs. After each session, ask:

- What did I do well?
- What lesson did I extract?
- How am I evolving?

You're not ignoring the mistakes—you're giving equal weight to growth. This balance builds confidence rooted in self-awareness, not perfection.

Final Word

Journaling isn't soft. It's strategic.

It's the difference between repeating the same year of trading ten times, or actually improving every quarter. Your journal is a microscope. Use it to dissect your decisions. Track the emotional data. Extract the edge hidden inside your own behavior.

When done right, journaling turns your past into your most powerful teacher.

Section 5: Emotional Capital Management

The Invisible Currency of Trading

Most traders think of capital in terms of money—account size, risk per trade, daily drawdown. But there's another form of capital that's even more important: your **emotional capital**.

This is the energy you use to stay patient, to think clearly, to hold a trade without panicking, to journal after a loss, to walk away after a win. It's your mental fuel. And like any fuel, it burns.

The traders who blow up don't just run out of money—they run out of clarity. Out of discipline. Out of focus. Because they never learned how to manage their emotional liquidity. That's what this section is about: protecting the mental bandwidth that actually sustains high-performance execution.

Your Brain Budget: Managing Mental Energy

Your brain has a budget—limited attention, limited willpower, limited clarity. Every decision, even small ones, burns part of that budget.

- Checking price ten times a minute? Burn.
- Hesitating on a setup? Burn.
- Regretting the last trade? Burn.
- Debating whether or not to enter? Burn.
- Switching systems mid-session? Burn.

If you don't manage your mental capital like you manage your money, you'll hit emotional drawdown faster than financial. And when that happens, you start trading from fatigue—not focus.

Track your brain budget. Know what drains you. Know what refuels you. Because your next win might depend more on your *mental state* than your market read.

Recharging Systems

What do you do to reset? If your only recovery tactic is stepping away, that's not a system—it's an escape.

You need proactive recharging habits. A real re-entry protocol that helps you return to the market *mentally fresh*.

Try:

- Breathing routines before each session
- Mid-session walks to reset attention
- Post-trade reflection rituals
- Weekly off-days with zero charts

This isn't laziness—it's fuel management. The market will always be there. But your ability to *see it clearly* depends on how well you protect your clarity.

Detachment Habits

Attachment is one of the biggest energy leaks in trading. You hold onto trades because you're attached to being right. You skip setups because you're still replaying the last mistake. You let a bad morning bleed into your afternoon because your mind hasn't detached.

Detachment is a skill. And like any skill, it needs training.

Build these habits:

- After every trade, say aloud: "That trade is over."
- After a loss, journal it, close the chart, walk away.
- After a win, delay checking the PnL.
- Use physical movement (a quick stretch, a step outside) to signal a reset.

These tiny rituals help you create *mental separation*—so you can step into each decision clean, not carrying the baggage of the last.

Momentum vs. Burnout Cycles

Momentum is powerful—when you manage it. If not, it can become emotional intoxication. You win a few trades and start feeling invincible. So you increase size, take lower-quality setups, and skip rituals. That's not momentum—that's a burnout trap.

The key is to harness momentum without letting it hijack your process. When you're in flow, double down on *discipline,* not just trades. Use hot streaks to reinforce good habits, not override them.

Likewise, during a losing streak, the emotional temptation is to "fix it" fast. Instead, slow down. Trade smaller. Take micro-wins. Focus on clean execution over PnL. That's how you survive drawdown without burning your identity.

Emotional Liquidity is Your Real Capital

At the end of the day, you can lose a trade and bounce back—if your emotional capital is still strong. But if you drain your mental reserves, even a small loss can spiral into overtrading, revenge, or paralysis.

Your job isn't just to manage financial risk. It's to protect the part of you that *executes* the plan. That's your emotional capital. That's your real currency.

Final Word

Great traders don't just manage accounts. They manage themselves.

Protect your mental energy like it's your trading balance. Because when emotional capital runs dry, no system, strategy, or setup can save you.

Just like a financial budget, you have a limited number of "mental dollars" to spend each day. Every chart flip, market scan, or hesitation burns some of that fuel. Smart traders know when to stop spending. Emotional bankruptcy happens not just from losing trades—but from too many small, careless decisions that slowly drain your system. Your edge isn't just what you do—but when you choose not to.

10 Hidden Tactics to Sharpen Your Internal Edge

These tactics weren't invented by me—they were collected. I've found them in trading books, deep-dive tutorials, YouTube videos, and the occasional private group or paid course. Some are well-hidden, others are just underused—but together, they form a playbook of practical, powerful ways to upgrade how you trade.

1. Post-Trade Hypnosis Anchoring

Use self-hypnosis or guided meditation immediately after a well-executed trade to reinforce calm, focused states. This conditions your subconscious to associate discipline with reward, making it easier to replicate under pressure.

2. Emotional Drawdown Tracker

Create a log to track emotional responses during trades—note feelings like fear, greed, or hesitation. Over time, identify patterns and develop strategies to manage these emotions effectively.

3. "Loss Lab" Review System

After each losing trade, analyze not just the technical aspects but also your emotional state and decision-making process. This helps in identifying recurring psychological pitfalls.

4. Bias Tracking Logs

Maintain a journal to record any biases influencing your trades, such as favoring certain assets or timeframes. Regularly reviewing this can help in mitigating subconscious influences.

5. Narrative Reframing in Trade Logs

Instead of labeling trades as "wins" or "losses," focus on adherence to your trading plan. This shift in perspective reinforces process over outcome.

6. Detachment Habits

Develop rituals to mentally separate from trades after execution, such as taking a short walk or practicing deep breathing. This prevents emotional carryover into subsequent trades.

7. Momentum vs. Burnout Cycles

Recognize the difference between productive momentum and overtrading. Implement scheduled breaks and limit consecutive trading days to maintain peak performance.

8. Confidence Recovery Rate

After a loss, measure how quickly you return to confident trading. Develop strategies, such as reviewing past successful trades, to expedite this recovery.

9. Process Scorecard Over PnL

At the end of each trading day, rate your adherence to your trading plan on a scale of 1-10. This emphasizes consistency and discipline over short-term profits.

10. Emotional Liquidity Management

Just as you manage financial capital, monitor your emotional energy. Avoid overtrading and ensure adequate rest to maintain mental clarity.

Final Thought

Mastering the internal edge is about consistent self-awareness and discipline. Implementing these tactics can lead to improved decision-making and long-term trading success.

CHAPTER 8

Tactical Mindset Frameworks

Rituals and systems that create emotional certainty on command.

If earlier chapters were about awareness, discipline, and internal structure, this one is about execution on a **tactical level**—turning those internal shifts into repeatable behaviors.

You can't control the market. You can't predict the next candle. But you *can* control your process. And that's what elite traders do—they create **systems for emotional certainty**. Not because they always feel good, but because they've trained themselves to act consistently *regardless* of how they feel.

That's what this chapter delivers.

We're going to build you five tactical frameworks—plug-and-play rituals that anchor you under pressure, center your focus, and create internal *precision* when the market gets noisy.

These aren't just ideas. These are drills. Daily practices. Mental checklists. Self-audits. Protocols you can use every single session to stabilize your emotions and lock in professional-level behavior.

Section 1: The Funded Five Protocol

Why This Protocol Matters

Most traders think they'll become consistent *after* they get funded. But the truth is, the market doesn't grant you capital to make you a professional—it gives you capital to reveal who you already are.

That's the philosophy behind the Funded Five Protocol.

It's a five-day challenge designed to simulate the pressure, focus, and precision of a real funded account—*before* you ever receive it. This isn't about testing your strategy. It's about testing your identity. Can you follow your rules with zero deviation? Can you execute like a funded trader before anyone hands you funding?

That's what separates traders who *get* funded from traders who *stay* funded.

Execute 5 Trades with Zero Deviation

For five days, your job is to take only five trades. One per day. That's it.

But here's the catch: **each trade must be executed with complete alignment to your plan**. No exceptions. You can't enter early. You can't skip journaling. You can't adjust your stop-loss based on feeling.

If a trade shows up and doesn't meet your criteria, you pass—even if it "looks good." If no trade shows up at all, you sit on your hands.

This is execution conditioning. You're rewiring yourself to prioritize *discipline over activity*—which is exactly what real capital requires.

Log Everything, Judge Nothing

The moment you enter the trade, your job shifts from "trader" to "observer."

You'll log:

- What you felt before entering
- What triggered your decision
- What your body did (tightness, rush, calm)
- What thoughts followed entry

And then you'll stop. No evaluation. No judgment. No obsessing over the result.

Why? Because the Funded Five Protocol isn't about outcome—it's about *self-witnessing*. You're training your brain to detach from win/loss thinking and lean into performance psychology.

This is where emotional clarity gets built.

Journal in Real-Time

Set a timer immediately after each trade ends—win or loss. Take 3–5 minutes to journal *in the moment,* not hours later when your emotions are faded or rewritten.

Write down:

- What did I do well?
- What tempted me to deviate?
- What would I do differently if this same setup appeared again?

Real-time journaling builds memory accuracy, emotional self-awareness, and mental honesty. It also prevents hindsight bias from corrupting your learning.

This is how you build *live feedback loops*—the fastest way to grow without needing more trades.

Create Pattern Recognition Rituals

After Day 3, you'll start to notice things: recurring thoughts, repeated emotions, setups that trigger fear, or behaviors that creep in post-trade.

This is gold.

Don't just notice it—*ritualize* it. Create a personal checklist of your top 3 psychological tendencies. Then, before each trade, review the list.

Example:

- "I tend to rush entries when I'm on a hot streak."
- "I overthink when there's high volatility."
- "I hesitate on clean setups after a red trade."

These micro-patterns shape your results. And once you recognize them, you can design pre-trade rituals to neutralize them.

Repeat for 5 Days: Track Identity Shifts

By the end of Day 5, you'll have something most traders never create: a map of how you behave under precision-based pressure.

You'll know:

- How you respond to rules
- How your ego reacts when forced to wait
- How your emotions fluctuate with small sample sizes
- How often you follow through when the outcome is uncertain

And most importantly—you'll feel the identity shift. You won't just *talk* like a pro. You'll have five days of proof that you can execute like one.

Final Word

The Funded Five isn't about passing a challenge. It's about becoming the kind of trader who doesn't need one to prove they belong. This protocol turns potential into process, and process into **identity**.

Section 2: The Stoic Stop-Loss System

Why Stop-Losses Trigger So Much Emotion

Every trader *says* they accept risk. Every strategy *includes* a stop-loss. But emotionally? Most traders don't believe the loss until it hits. And when it does, it feels personal. Frustrating. Maybe even embarrassing.

You click out—or worse, get stopped out—and suddenly your mind spins: *Why did I take that? Should I have waited? Maybe the market is rigged.* That's not rational thinking. That's a nervous system in threat mode.

Loss triggers fear because we've been conditioned to associate it with failure. But in trading, loss is not only normal—it's **built in**. The market will test your tolerance, your self-worth, your confidence. And your job is to train a mindset that treats stop-losses not as punishment, but as **data points on your growth curve**.

That's what the Stoic Stop-Loss System is designed to do.

Assign Meaning to Every Stop Hit

Your first step is reframing. Every time you take a stop, you must *assign meaning*—not emotionally, but intentionally.

Ask:

- Did this loss come from a rule-following trade?
- Did I execute with integrity?
- What market behavior caused the invalidation?

By asking these questions, you extract the lesson from the experience. Instead of reacting with frustration or avoidance, you engage with curiosity. You're not just a trader anymore—you're a student of *yourself* and your process.

Over time, this rewiring turns losses into neutral events. Just like a basketball player missing a shot they were trained to take—it's not a failure. It's a necessary part of the volume.

Build a Rule-Respect Muscle

There's a specific pain that comes from taking a loss *you weren't supposed to take*. A rushed entry. A trade too large. A setup you knew wasn't clean.

That pain isn't from the loss—it's from the *broken agreement with yourself*.

You can eliminate 80% of emotional damage from losses just by tightening your respect for rules. Every time you follow your plan—even if it ends in red—you're building **identity capital**. You're telling your brain: "We keep our word. We operate with structure."

That's how confidence is built.

Create a simple "Rule Respect Score" after every trade:

- Did I follow my entry checklist?
- Did I size appropriately?
- Did I follow exit criteria, not emotion?

Rate yourself 1–5. Track it weekly. The goal is to get to a place where following rules becomes more satisfying than winning trades.

The "Pain Rehearsal" Pre-Trade Exercise

Before you enter a trade, take 30 seconds to mentally rehearse the stop-out.

Visualize the trade going against you. Imagine the red. Feel the loss. Then say out loud:

> "If this trade hits stop-loss and I followed my plan, it is a win."

This single exercise trains your mind to expect discomfort without resistance. It removes the element of surprise. It conditions emotional neutrality before emotional activation even begins.

You're no longer caught off guard by the worst-case scenario—because you already made peace with it.

Emotional Journaling After Loss

Right after a stop-out, set a 3-minute timer and journal these prompts:

- What am I feeling right now?
- Did I follow my process?
- What belief is trying to take over?

This slows down the impulse loop. It brings awareness to emotional hijacks. And over time, it helps you see that the post-loss spiral isn't about the market—it's about the *story* you're attaching to it.

Detach the story, and the loss loses its power.

Rewire: Pain = Progress

Here's the ultimate Stoic shift: **Pain is not the enemy. It's the signal that you're refining.**

If you're never feeling discomfort, you're probably not evolving. You're playing safe, avoiding risk, or trading from fear. But if you're following your system, executing with precision, and still hitting losses—that's not regression. That's growth.

You don't become resilient by avoiding red. You become resilient by walking through red with composure and process.

Final Word

Stop-losses aren't losses. They're tuition. They're the cost of doing business. They're feedback loops designed to sharpen your edge—*if you're mentally trained to receive them.*

Use this system to stay calm, consistent, and composed—no matter what the next candle brings.

Section 3: Dopamine Discipline Rituals

Why Dopamine Is Quietly Driving Your Worst Trades

You probably think your mistakes come from fear, impatience, or lack of discipline. But under the surface, many of them are driven by something more primal: **dopamine mismanagement**.

Dopamine is the brain's reward chemical. It's what pushes you to seek novelty, chase pleasure, and avoid discomfort. In trading, it fuels the rush of entering a position, the itch to "just click," the thrill of watching price move—even if it's not your setup.

The problem? Trading success requires doing the **opposite** of what dopamine wants. You have to sit through boredom. Wait for your edge. Take small, repetitive actions. And often, you must delay gratification for days or weeks.

So how do you trade in a dopamine-addicted environment without becoming a dopamine-addicted trader?

You rewire your system—with *rituals designed to train emotional neutrality and long-game behavior.*

The Cold Click Method

This is a ritual for mastering emotionally uncomfortable trades—the ones that meet your criteria but "don't feel good." Maybe it's after a loss, or when the market's choppy, or when you're second-guessing your edge.

When that setup shows up, and it fits your rules, *you take it cold.*

You don't wait for confidence. You don't hope for confirmation bias. You click, and then you walk away.

This method builds the muscle of **process over emotion**. It teaches your brain to prioritize logic, not safety. The more you do it, the less you need to "feel ready" to act—and the more consistently you'll trade through discomfort.

No-Trade Challenge (Sit With Silence)

Set a day where your only goal is to **not trade at all**—even if setups appear. This isn't laziness. It's discipline training.

Throughout the session:

- Watch the market with intention.
- Journal your thoughts as trades appear.
- Notice your urges to act.
- Do nothing.

This challenge rewires your relationship with **stillness**. It shows you that action isn't always value, and silence doesn't equal missed opportunity.

By learning to sit in the tension of boredom, you build the psychological gap between *impulse and action*—and that gap is where professional discipline lives.

Delayed Gratification Journal

After each trade, delay checking your PnL for **10 minutes**. Use that time to journal:

- Did I follow my plan?

- How clean was my execution?
- What would I do differently next time?

This ritual trains you to value **process quality over result**. The delay breaks the dopamine loop of "click, win, feel good" or "click, lose, panic."

Eventually, your brain begins to crave *clean execution* as its own reward—because that's where your self-respect is built.

Reward System Reinforcement

Here's the twist: dopamine isn't the enemy. It just needs to be **reassigned**.

Instead of letting it reward random behavior, use it to reinforce **discipline**. Create a system:

- Journaling = 1 point
- Rule-following = 2 points
- Clean stop-loss with zero reaction = 3 points
- Full session without deviation = 5 points

Then assign rewards:

- 25 points = favorite snack
- 50 points = one Netflix episode
- 100 points = day off or small purchase

This reprograms your brain to associate *pleasure* with the *process*, not just the outcome. Over time, the habit loop shifts in your favor.

Weekly Wins Reflection Ritual

Every Friday, before you shut the charts, sit down and reflect on your **behavioral wins**—not just your trading ones.

Ask:

- When did I act like the trader I want to become?
- When did I overcome emotion?
- What system did I follow that used to trip me up?

Write them down. Celebrate them.

Why? Because consistency requires reinforcement. If you don't pause to recognize your growth, your brain will only track your PnL—and that's a guaranteed dopamine trap.

Final Word

You're not just fighting your emotions—you're rewiring your reward system. Dopamine discipline rituals turn trading into a game of focus, patience, and internal mastery.

Win that game, and the market starts to feel less like a casino—and more like a *mirror of your consistency*.

Section 4: The 5-Day Funded Simulation

Why You Must Practice Under Pressure Before It's Real

Most traders think the moment they "get funded," everything will magically click. Their discipline will improve. Their execution will sharpen. Their results will stabilize. But here's the truth: **funding doesn't change you—it exposes you.**

If your habits are shaky, capital magnifies the cracks. If your emotions are untrained, pressure will trigger chaos. The market won't give you more time to evolve just because there's more money on the line.

That's why this simulation exists.

The 5-Day Funded Simulation is a mental stress test. It puts your identity, habits, and focus under **simulated pressure** so that when the real capital arrives, your process doesn't break.

Many professional traders run multiple accounts at once—whether managing client money, prop firm capital, or personal strategies. Consistency across platforms is critical here: one slip and the whole structure unravels.

Back in 2010, I built a tool to solve that problem: Local Trade Copier (mt4copier.com). It lets me open, adjust, and close trades simultaneously across dozens of MT4/MT5 accounts—without copy & paste errors, mismatched sizes, or timing delays. It's not rocket science—just precise execution at scale.

Think of it this way: having a trade copier is like giving yourself a system that never gets tired, never makes impulsive mistakes, and always follows your exact risk plan. It's not about being flashy—it's about being reliable.

You don't have to use it—and many traders don't. But understanding that real fund managers operate this way can help shift your mindset from *"I might trade well today"* to *"I can deliver consistent, replicable execution, account after account."*

Simulate Real Capital Conditions

Pick a trading account—demo, micro, or live—with a balance that **feels emotionally significant.** It doesn't have to be a huge number, but it should carry some weight. Enough that your decisions feel serious, not disposable.

Then, for five consecutive trading days, act as if:

- You've been given a real six-figure account.
- Every trade must be executed by the book.
- Your job is on the line—not based on profits, but based on **discipline.**

This isn't roleplay. It's **identity rehearsal**.

Your goal is to match your behavior to your future self—the funded, stable, professional version of you.

Obey Rules Without Exception

During the simulation, your system rules are law. You don't break them—not for a "good-looking setup," not for FOMO, not because "this one's different."

This forces your brain into process-first thinking. It teaches you to trust your framework, not your feelings.

It also exposes where your real weaknesses are:

- Do you rush entries under pressure?
- Do you skip journaling when tired?
- Do you loosen stops when you're losing?

The simulation makes those patterns obvious—so you can *fix them before they cost you real capital.*

Accountability Partner or Group

Pressure without accountability becomes a game. You'll bend your rules if no one knows. That's why this works best when someone is watching—or reviewing.

Find a partner, mentor, or group. Share your daily plan and post-simulation review. Report:

- What trades you took (with screenshots)
- How closely you followed your plan
- What emotional patterns came up
- What you'll refine tomorrow

This adds *healthy pressure*—not to perform perfectly, but to stay honest. Because private discipline is hard to measure. But shared discipline builds *reputation-backed consistency.*

Emotional Trade Flagging System

Every trade during the simulation should be tagged based on emotional influence:

- Green = Clean execution, no emotion
- Yellow = Emotional presence, still followed plan
- Red = Emotion overruled process

At the end of each day, log your ratio. This is your **emotional execution score**.

It has nothing to do with PnL—and everything to do with who you are under pressure. And over time, as you lower your Red trades and increase your Greens, you build something more powerful than accuracy: *emotional reliability.*

Trade Like You're Auditioning

Here's the mental reframe that changes everything:

> "This isn't just a simulation. This is an audition."

Act like your trades are being reviewed by a prop firm. Like someone is watching how you think, how you wait, how you react. Not to judge your profits—but to measure your *professionalism.*

That kind of awareness upgrades every action.

You don't click recklessly when you're being watched. You don't abandon your rules when your reputation's on the line. You trade cleaner, sharper, slower—and those habits become **your new normal.**

Final Word

The 5-Day Funded Simulation trains you to behave like the trader you say you want to be—*before* the capital shows up.

Because getting funded doesn't turn you into a pro.

Acting like a pro is what gets you—and keeps you—funded.

Section 5: MAPS System: Your North Star

Why You Need a Daily Compass

Trading without a mental compass is like sailing without a map. You might feel in control, but the moment the wind shifts—news, volatility, a losing streak—you drift. Fast. And often without even realizing it.

The MAPS System gives you a **five-point mental checklist** to guide your focus, align your actions, and protect your psychology. It's not a motivational tool—it's a **navigation system**. A ritual that brings your scattered energy back into structure before every session.

MAPS stands for:

- **Mindset**
- **Accountability**
- **Patience**
- **Structure**
- **Execution**

Let's break each one down.

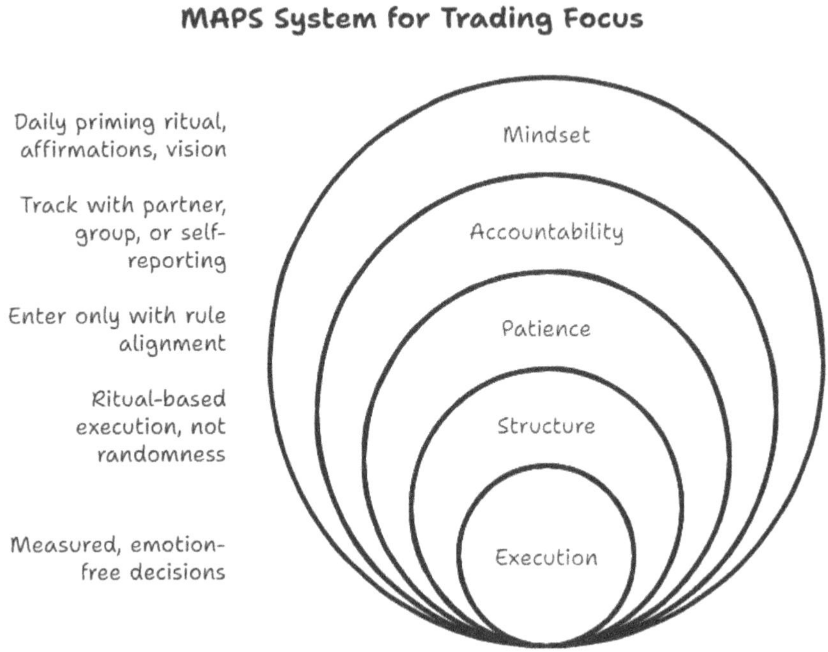

Mindset (Daily Priming)

Your mindset is the lens through which you interpret everything. A clean trade taken in a panicked headspace becomes self-sabotage. A minor loss in a strong mindset becomes a lesson.

Before every session, prime your mindset intentionally:

- What energy are you bringing into the day?
- What do you need to let go of from yesterday?
- Are you trading from pressure—or purpose?

Use a one-minute morning script. Say it out loud or write it down:

> "Today I trade my plan, not my feelings. I focus on process, not outcomes. I'm here to execute like the trader I'm becoming."

This isn't fluff. It's **preloading your system with clarity**.

Accountability (Public or Peer)

Discipline dies in isolation. When no one's watching, you start breaking rules, stretching limits, and "justifying" behaviors you swore you'd outgrown.

Add light accountability to your daily trading. That could mean:

- Sending your daily plan to a trading buddy
- Reviewing trades in a weekly group
- Posting a "no trade taken today" recap to a journal channel

The point isn't exposure—it's *pressure*. A soft layer of expectation that reminds you: **someone's paying attention**. And if no one else is, *you* are.

Traders who win long-term don't just track performance—they stay *accountable to behavior.*

Patience (Defined Conditions Only)

Impatience is the root of most blown accounts. It turns "wait for the setup" into "this kinda looks good." It turns boredom into overtrading. And it always feels justified in the moment.

The fix? Define your **readiness conditions** before you trade:

- What specific price action or indicator behavior triggers your setup?
- What time of day is optimal for you?
- When *shouldn't* you trade?

List them clearly before the session. And if those conditions don't appear? You don't trade. Period.

This removes ambiguity—and ambiguity is the enemy of patience.

Structure (Ritual Over Randomness)

Most traders jump into the market like it's social media—scrolling, reacting, clicking. That's randomness. And randomness breeds emotional chaos.

Structure is what makes elite behavior **repeatable**. It removes the need for willpower by making consistency automatic.

Use this basic ritual framework:

- Morning prep (chart markups, mindset script)
- Pre-trade checklist
- Post-trade journal (win or lose)
- End-of-day scorecard

Stick to this structure. Adjust the details if you need—but don't improvise the process. Your edge isn't just in your strategy—it's in your *rituals*.

Execution (Measured, Not Emotional)

At the end of the day, none of this matters if you can't click with calm.

Your execution must be:

- Slow
- Clean
- Detached from outcome
- Rooted in your system—not your mood

Before you place any trade, ask:

> "Am I executing this from structure—or emotion?"

This one question can prevent 80% of your bad trades.

Execution isn't about confidence. It's about *control*. The trader who learns to click with neutrality—win or lose—is the one who earns consistency.

Final Word: MAPS = Mental GPS

You don't need to feel amazing every day. You don't need perfect focus or perfect setups. What you need is a **reliable compass**—a way to re-center yourself when things get fast, emotional, or overwhelming.

That's what MAPS does. It pulls you back to *process over panic*. It gives you a framework to act like a pro even when your emotions are begging you to act like a beginner.

Use it daily. Review it weekly. Live it until it becomes default.

Because when the market gets loud, the quiet power of your inner structure is what keeps you profitable.

10 Tactical Mindset Hacks for Elite Traders

These tactics come from books, tutorials, videos, and the occasional private group. I've collected what works—not what's trendy—to give you tools you can apply right now, before you're funded. Some are overlooked. A few are even a little gray hat.

1. Neuro-Priming with Anchored Triggers

Pair a specific physical action (e.g., tapping your wrist) with a calming phrase like "I trade my plan" during moments of clarity. Repeating this consistently conditions your nervous system to associate the action with a focused state, enabling rapid emotional resets during trading.

2. Sensory Deprivation Pre-Session

Before trading, spend 10 minutes in a dark, quiet room or use a blindfold and noise-canceling headphones. This sensory deprivation reduces external stimuli, allowing you to center your focus and enter a heightened state of awareness, similar to techniques used by elite athletes.

3. Micro-Dosing Market Exposure

Limit your screen time to specific intervals (e.g., 15 minutes every hour) to prevent overexposure and maintain mental freshness. This approach helps in reducing decision fatigue and promotes more deliberate trading actions.

4. Emotional Calibration with Music

Create playlists that evoke specific emotional states—calmness, aggression, focus—and use them strategically during trading sessions to modulate your emotional state and maintain optimal arousal levels.

5. Reverse Journaling

Instead of journaling after trades, write down your emotional and mental state before entering a trade. This proactive approach increases self-awareness and can help in identifying patterns that lead to suboptimal decisions.

6. Gamified Discipline Tracking

Implement a point-based system to reward adherence to trading rules (e.g., +1 for following the plan, -1 for deviations). Accumulated points can be exchanged for small rewards, reinforcing disciplined behavior through gamification.

7. Visualization of Worst-Case Scenarios

Regularly visualize potential losses and how you would handle them calmly. This mental rehearsal prepares you for adverse outcomes, reducing fear and emotional reactivity when they occur.

8. Delayed Gratification Exercises

After a successful trade, delay checking your profits for a set period (e.g., 30 minutes). This practice trains you to detach from immediate rewards and focus on the process rather than outcomes.

9. Accountability Partnerships

Partner with another trader to review each other's trades and adherence to rules. This external accountability can enhance discipline and provide new perspectives on your trading behavior.

10. Use of Biofeedback Devices

Employ biofeedback tools (e.g., heart rate monitors) to gain real-time insights into your physiological state. Monitoring these signals can help you recognize stress responses early and implement calming techniques promptly.

Final Note

These strategies are designed to enhance your trading mindset and discipline. While some may push the boundaries of conventional practices, ensure they align with ethical standards and personal values. Always test new techniques in a controlled environment before full implementation.

CHAPTER 9

The Contract Code

Turn identity into obligation. Turn discipline into your default.

At some point, discipline must stop being a goal—and start being a **standard**. That shift doesn't come from motivation or inspiration. It comes from **commitment engineering**.

This chapter is about turning your trading identity into a living contract. A system of *behavioral boundaries, daily pledges, environmental triggers, and public accountability* that remove willpower from the equation.

When you make your process sacred—ritualized, witnessed, reinforced—you don't have to "feel ready." You *are ready,* because your systems are stronger than your moods.

This is the Contract Code: a tactical blueprint to turn your best trading self into a daily, repeatable habit.

Section 1: Behavioral Commitment Contracts

Why Discipline Needs a Contract, Not a Mood

The biggest mistake traders make is waiting to "feel" disciplined. They hope that with time, experience, or enough wins, discipline will just settle in like muscle memory.

But discipline doesn't come from time. It comes from **structure**. More specifically, it comes from commitment frameworks—boundaries that turn intention into behavior, and behavior into identity.

Enter: **Behavioral Commitment Contracts.**

These aren't metaphorical. You're going to write your own. Review it daily. Sign it. Live it. Because when you build a personal trading contract rooted in your *values and vision,* you no longer rely on emotion. You create **a code**—and that code becomes your edge.

Create Your Non-Negotiables

Start by defining your non-negotiables. These are not goals. These are not preferences. These are your *behavioral absolutes*—the rules you will not break, regardless of what the market does or how you feel.

Ask yourself:

- What behaviors destroy my consistency?
- What actions always lead to regret?
- What habits separate me from my highest-level self?

Now translate those answers into firm commitments. Example:

- "I do not trade without a pre-market ritual."

- "I do not increase position size mid-trade."
- "I do not skip journaling under any circumstance."

Write 5–10 of these. Keep them visible. They are your new trading laws.

Public Declarations & Peer Witnessing

It's easy to lie to yourself. It's harder to lie when someone's watching.

Once your non-negotiables are set, **declare them publicly**—to a trading partner, a community, or a journal group. Let someone else *witness your code.*

This single action adds healthy pressure. When your commitment is known, your standards rise. You're no longer "hoping to be consistent"—you've *declared* consistency, and others expect it.

This doesn't mean you're seeking approval. It means you're using **visibility as leverage** against self-sabotage.

The Written Edge Agreement

Now it's time to formalize your contract. Write it like a legal document. Sign it. Date it. Treat it like a business owner would treat their operating agreement.

Include:

- Your Non-Negotiables
- Your Trading Philosophy in 3–5 sentences
- Your Reason for Trading (beyond money)
- The Identity You Are Committed to Becoming

- A Statement of Consequence (what happens when you break the contract)

Here's a sample intro:

> "I, [Name], commit to the standards of execution and mindset outlined in this agreement. This contract exists to protect my edge, my evolution, and the trader I am becoming. I will act in alignment, even when it's hard, because that's who I am training myself to be."

Review this Edge Agreement every week. It's your mirror. Not just for performance, but for *personal truth.*

Penalty & Reward System

Accountability without consequence is a theory. You need real stakes.

Every time you break your contract, there must be a cost. This isn't about punishment—it's about reinforcing *importance.*

Create a personal consequence system:

- Monetary Penalty: $5–$20 per violation into a "Discipline Jar."
- Time Penalty: Lose 30 minutes of personal screen time or Netflix.
- Physical Reps: 50 push-ups or 5 minutes of cold exposure.

On the flip side, reward clean streaks:

- 5 days of full alignment = small reward
- 10 days = something meaningful
- 30 days = major upgrade or experience

This anchors discipline in a feedback loop. You're not just *trying* to follow rules—you're living in a system that *reinforces them daily.*

The Honor Ritual

Once your contract is written and witnessed, seal it with an **Honor Ritual**. Something small but symbolic that marks this transition.

Some options:

- Light a candle and read the contract aloud.
- Print and sign it with a real pen.
- Record yourself reading it and listen before each trading week.
- Store it in a place of meaning—next to your setup, in a journal, on your lock screen.

This ritual is the mental handshake between who you've been—and who you're becoming.

Final Word:

Discipline is self-trust in action. Every time you follow through on your trading rules—even when it doesn't matter to anyone else—you build a reputation with yourself. That reputation is your real edge. The trader who keeps their own word, even in silence, becomes dangerous—because they no longer need external validation to execute with power.

A Behavioral Commitment Contract is more than paper. It's a decision. It's the line between "I want to be consistent" and "I *am* consistent—because I've built the structure to support it."

This is how you stop relying on emotion and start living your edge—*on purpose, every session.*

Section 2: The Daily Execution Pledge

Why Daily Identity Alignment Matters

Discipline isn't a switch you flip—it's a rhythm you rehearse. The most consistent traders don't "hope" they'll be focused each day. They *engineer* it.

This is what the Daily Execution Pledge is all about: aligning your identity before you click a single button. Before your eyes hit the charts, your *mind* needs to know what it stands for. Who you're showing up as. What kind of trader you're committed to being—regardless of market conditions, emotions, or previous outcomes.

This system combines intentional priming, visualization, and a simple execution score to turn each session into a **mental reset and recommitment**.

Let's break it down.

Morning Identity Statement

Your first task each day is to remind yourself of who you are becoming. Not your past trades. Not your current account balance. But your *trading identity*—the version of you that trades with structure, emotional clarity, and professional behavior.

Write or speak a short identity statement before each session. This can evolve, but it should hit three targets:

1. Who you are (identity)
2. How you act (behavior)
3. Why it matters (purpose)

Example:

> "I am a calm, focused trader. I follow my plan no matter what the market does. I'm here to build skill, not chase wins."

Saying this aloud isn't cheesy—it's **neural priming**. It fires the beliefs and intentions that create behavioral follow-through. Do it before you open your charts, every single session.

Pre-Market Visualizations

Next, spend 2–3 minutes mentally walking through your ideal trading behaviors. Close your eyes. Picture:

- Sitting calmly at your desk
- Executing only when your criteria is met
- Walking away from noise
- Journaling with clarity after each trade
- Taking a loss and responding with zero reaction

This isn't daydreaming. It's **mental rehearsal**.

Athletes do this before big games. Performers do it before shows. You're doing it to align your nervous system before stress hits.

Visualizing success *in advance* increases your ability to act in alignment *under pressure*. It turns intention into muscle memory.

End-of-Day Rituals

What happens *after* the trade is just as important as what happens before. The Daily Execution Pledge isn't complete until you close the loop with reflection.

Create a consistent post-market ritual:

- Log each trade (entry, exit, result, emotion)
- Review your process, not your profits
- Celebrate behavior that matched your code
- Extract one lesson—just one

Keep it short, but sacred. This ritual turns every session into a learning session. And more importantly, it reminds your subconscious: *we close clean.*

When you bookend your trading day with intention and reflection, your performance sharpens naturally.

Execution Score Review

At the end of each session, rate yourself on five categories:

1. Rule adherence
2. Emotional control
3. Patience
4. Setup quality
5. Post-trade behavior

Use a 1–10 scale. This becomes your **behavioral PnL**—a far more accurate measure of growth than your equity curve alone.

Optional: set a baseline. For example, "I will not consider the week successful unless I average an 8 or higher across all five metrics." This flips your goal from *winning* to *executing like a professional.*

Optional: Accountability Buddy Debrief

Want to supercharge this process? Share your execution pledge and scores with a trading partner. A quick 5-minute debrief call or message exchange:

- "Here's how I rated myself today."
- "Here's what I did well."
- "Here's where I slipped—and what I'll fix tomorrow."

It's not about being perfect. It's about being **present**—with your process, your identity, and your evolution.

Final Word:

The market won't wait for you to "get in the zone." It will test you the second you show up. The Daily Execution Pledge ensures that when that test comes, you've already chosen who you are and how you'll respond.

Don't leave your trading day to chance. Start it with intention. End it with reflection. That's how you turn scattered action into *elite-level consistency.*

Section 3: Ritual Design System

Why Rituals Are More Powerful Than Willpower

Ambition will get you excited. Rituals will keep you consistent.

The reality is that trading isn't hard because of technical complexity—it's hard because of mental inconsistency. You know your setup. You know your rules. But some days you follow them, and some days you don't.

Why?

Because you're relying on *willpower*. And willpower is a limited resource. It weakens under fatigue, stress, boredom, and ego. Rituals, on the other hand, don't ask how you feel. They don't care what kind of day you're having. Rituals are automatic. And *automation* is the key to making discipline your default.

This is where the Ritual Design System comes in—a framework to turn your trading process into a repeatable flow that runs on structure, not mood.

Study your own energy curve. For me, 80% of my cleanest trades came within the first two hours of the session. Beyond that, decision quality dropped. Know your window. Design your trading plan around it—not against it.

Stack Triggers and Anchors

The most powerful rituals begin *before* the work. You don't just open charts—you *prime your brain* to operate at peak focus.

Start by creating **triggers**—specific cues that tell your brain, "It's time to trade like a pro." These can be:

- Lighting a candle
- Playing a specific instrumental playlist
- Sipping coffee from the same mug
- Opening your journal and writing your identity statement

Then attach **anchors**—habits you consistently pair with those triggers. For example:

- Trigger: Start music → Anchor: Begin pre-market chart review
- Trigger: Open trading journal → Anchor: Review yesterday's execution score

Over time, these paired actions become muscle memory. Your mind doesn't ask, "Should I focus today?" It simply responds, "This is what we do now."

Use Environment as a Mindset Lever

Where you trade affects how you trade. Your environment can either distract you or support you. That's why top performers across disciplines—from athletes to CEOs—craft *intentional spaces*.

Audit your trading setup:

- Is it clean or cluttered?
- Do you have visual noise (social media tabs, notifications)?
- Is there anything within reach that pulls your attention away?

Now optimize it:

- Remove unnecessary tabs, icons, or tools
- Add visual anchors (your Edge Agreement, MAPS System, motivational quote)
- Use separate devices if needed: one for trading, one for everything else

Your environment should whisper, "Focus. Discipline. Identity." every time you sit down.

Automate First 15 Minutes of Market Open

The first 15 minutes after the market opens are where most traders lose composure. Volatility spikes. FOMO floods in. Structure collapses.

Solve this by creating a fixed **15-minute ritual** that you follow *every single day*. Examples:

- 5 minutes: Observe price action without trading
- 5 minutes: Recheck pre-market zones and key levels
- 5 minutes: Review mental checklist and state rating

This routine acts as a **buffer zone** between emotion and execution. It gives your rational brain time to take the wheel before you act on impulse.

It's not about avoiding trades—it's about building momentum from *stillness, not chaos.*

Lock in Your Focus Window

Decide in advance: when are you most focused? For most traders, it's not all day. Trying to be locked in for 8 hours straight leads to fatigue, sloppy trades, and emotional exhaustion.

Instead, block your **focus window**:

- Example: 8:00–10:00 AM only
- During that time: Full presence, no distractions, no multitasking
- Outside that time: Review, journal, walk, recharge

Boundaries create freedom. When your brain knows there's a set time to perform, it shows up sharper. You're training **intentional intensity**—not endless screen-staring.

Build Rituals That Signal Game Time

Every performer has a pre-game ritual. So should you. Your ritual doesn't need to be fancy. It just needs to be *yours*—reliable, repeatable, and meaningful.

Design your Game Time Sequence:

1. Brew coffee and sit with intention
2. Read your trading contract or identity statement
3. Light a candle or start your playlist
4. Review yesterday's best behavior
5. Open charts—calm, clear, focused

That sequence, repeated daily, becomes a mental anchor. It tells your nervous system: *We're not here to gamble. We're here to execute.*

Final Word:

You don't need more willpower. You need better rituals. Because under pressure, you won't rise to the level of your ambition—you'll fall to the level of your systems.

So build rituals that serve your edge. Protect your process with structure. And start each day knowing: *this is already decided.*

Section 4: Identity Reinforcement Tools

Why Identity Is the Foundation of Behavior

You don't become consistent by forcing yourself to act disciplined—you become consistent by *believing* that's who you are. In trading, behavior follows belief. Every hesitation, every revenge trade, every rule break isn't just a discipline issue—it's an **identity leak**.

If you still see yourself as "trying to get good at trading," you'll make decisions that reflect doubt. If you *believe* you're a disciplined, structured, professional trader—even if the results haven't caught up yet—you'll behave in alignment with that belief.

The tools in this section are designed to reinforce your identity from the inside out. You'll be using intention, visualization, written contracts, and weekly reflections to anchor the version of yourself you're committed to becoming.

The One-Sentence Identity Challenge

Clarity breeds consistency. Start each week by writing a single sentence that captures who you are as a trader. Not your stats. Not your hopes. Your **identity**.

Examples:

- "I am a calm, focused sniper who follows process over emotion."
- "I am a professional who shows up with structure, no matter the outcome."
- "I am a funded-level executor, even when no one's watching."

Read this sentence every morning before your session. Tape it to your monitor. Whisper it before each entry. The more often your brain sees it, the more likely it is to align your behavior with it.

This is self-conditioning, not fluff. Identity is programmable—and repetition is the code.

The Professional Avatar Exercise

Here's a question: If you were already a full-time, successful, respected, fully funded trader—how would you behave *differently*?

Would you:

- Rush into trades?
- Skip your journal?
- Keep overleveraging?
- Panic on a stop-loss?

Probably not.

Create a mental model of your **Professional Avatar**. Visualize them:

- How they sit at the desk
- How they wait for trades
- How they speak to themselves after a loss
- How they show up every day—no excuses

Then ask: *What would that version of me do right now?*

This one shift kills self-sabotage fast. Because it gives you a role to step into—*not based on outcome, but on identity.*

Future-Self Contract

Write a letter or short contract from your **future self**—the version of you who is consistent, confident, and making real money with real discipline.

It might start like this:

> "Hey. I'm writing to you from six months ahead. I'm the version of you that finally stopped overtrading, stopped chasing, and started following the damn plan. It wasn't easy. But it was worth it…"

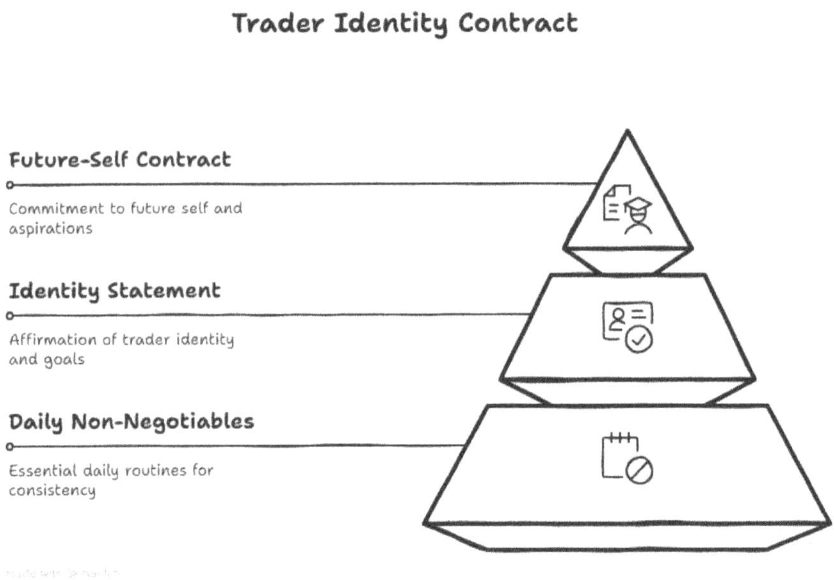

Outline:

- What habits this future-you sticks to
- What they've stopped doing
- How they handle bad trades, FOMO, and emotional days
- What's changed—internally and externally

Print it. Sign it. Keep it nearby. This isn't just motivation—it's a **north star** for your daily behavior.

Journaling to Remember Who You Are

After tough sessions, identity can get blurry. You start questioning your ability, your system, your journey. That's when journaling becomes a weapon—not just a reflection.

Use this two-part identity journal prompt:

1. *"What did I do today that aligned with the trader I want to be?"*
2. *"What identity did I act from when I slipped—and what triggered it?"*

This keeps your self-perception clear. You're not "good or bad." You're either aligned with your identity—or drifting from it. And both give you data to grow.

Habit Reflection Weekly Scan

Once a week, scan your behavior through the lens of identity. Not outcomes. Not stats. Just *who you were being.*

Questions to ask:

- What behavior did I repeat that my future self would be proud of?
- What habits need reinforcement?
- What am I still doing that belongs to the old version of me?

This scan keeps you honest. It prevents drift. And it reminds you: **trading success isn't a technical milestone—it's an identity evolution.**

Final Word:

You're not trying to act like a pro trader. You're **becoming** one. And becoming starts with belief.

Use these identity tools daily. Train your mind to see yourself as someone worth trusting. Because once you do, your actions will follow—and the market will start reflecting who you truly are.

Section 5: Accountability Frameworks

Why Accountability Accelerates Evolution

Discipline in private is powerful—but discipline with accountability is *unbreakable.*

Most traders operate in isolation. They build systems, make promises to themselves, and hope they'll follow through. But without any external structure, those promises weaken. Slowly at first. Then all at once.

Accountability adds tension to your commitment—in a good way. It makes your private discipline **publicly visible**, which adds a layer of integrity that most traders never access. You stop saying, *"I'll try,"* and start living, *"I gave my word."*

This section gives you tools to build your own accountability ecosystem—so your growth isn't just self-powered, but **community-supported**.

Daily Micro-Wins

Big goals collapse under pressure. Micro-wins build momentum. And accountability thrives when there's daily proof of progress.

Create a Micro-Wins Tracking Sheet. Each day, your only job is to log 1–3 small victories. Examples:

- Followed your pre-trade checklist
- Waited out a mediocre setup
- Took a clean loss without emotional reaction
- Journaled within 15 minutes of your final trade

These don't need to be dramatic. The key is consistency. Small wins, tracked daily, send your brain one powerful message: *"I'm doing this."*

Share your micro-wins with a peer or small group. Not for praise—but for **pattern recognition and proof of alignment**.

30-Day Execution Challenge

If you want to hardwire new behavior, create a 30-day challenge—not based on profit, but on *execution quality*.

Rules:

- Choose 3–5 core behaviors (ex: no trades without checklist, pre-session journaling, fixed position size)
- Follow them daily, no exceptions
- Score yourself each day: ✅ or ❌
- Post your score to a partner or group every 5 days

Optional: add a consequence if you break the streak. Maybe you donate to a cause you dislike or restart the clock. The point isn't punishment—it's **performance pressure with integrity**.

This challenge rewires your brain for identity-aligned behavior. Not based on how you feel. Based on **what you said you would do.**

Trader Scorecard & Dashboard

To stay on mission, you need a scoreboard—not for PnL, but for *personal execution.*

Create a weekly scorecard with categories like:

- Rule adherence (1–10)
- Emotional control (1–10)
- Ritual consistency (1–10)
- Post-trade journaling (1–10)
- Self-review and improvement (1–10)

Review each category every Friday. Total your score. Track your averages weekly.

Now here's the upgrade: **make your dashboard visible to your accountability partner or group.** If your numbers drop, they'll see it—and ask why. That pressure isn't to shame you. It's to *support you through the inconsistency you might ignore alone.*

Group Review & Rituals

Solo growth works… until it doesn't. Eventually, you need a mirror. A circle. A small group of like-minded traders with one goal: *evolve together.*

Here's how to build or join a **Discipline Circle**:

- Meet once a week (Zoom or chat group)
- Everyone shares one win, one struggle, one focus for next week
- Keep it short: 30–60 minutes max
- No advice unless requested. Just reflection and support.

The goal is rhythm and **collective pressure**. When you're not the only one holding the line, the line becomes easier to hold.

If you don't have a circle, start one. One person is enough. Invite a peer who respects discipline over hype. Grow slowly. Protect the culture.

Build or Join a Discipline Circle

Discipline Circles aren't about sharing setups. They're about sharing *standards*.

Set core agreements:

- This group is for behavior, not bragging
- Results are secondary to execution
- Vulnerability is welcome—because honesty fuels growth

Use shared scoreboards. Run group 30-day challenges. Cheer micro-wins. Call out drift. The power of the Discipline Circle is this: *when one of us rises, we all rise.*

Final Word:

Accountability turns your commitment into a contract. It transforms discipline from a personal struggle into a shared pursuit. And when you surround yourself with people who expect your best—you start living up to it.

Trading may be a solo game. But mastery is a **team pursuit**.

Takeaway Principle:

"Discipline isn't something you feel. It's something you've agreed to."

This is the core truth of The Contract Code.

You don't rise in trading because you're in the mood. You rise because you've made **a decision**—and then built the **structure** to protect it.
It's not enough to *want* to be consistent. You need to **engineer consistency into your system**. You need contracts, rituals, pledges, reviews, and accountability layers that keep your identity locked in—even when the market throws chaos your way.

Because chaos is coming.

You will lose trades. You will feel off. You will want to break your own rules.

The question is: *Have you created a system that still holds you in place when you feel like unraveling?*

That's what this chapter has given you:

- A behavioral contract to solidify your edge
- Daily pledges to prime execution
- Ritual systems to eliminate emotional drift
- Identity tools to act like your future self *now*
- Accountability structures that create external alignment

When you layer these together, your performance becomes *unshakeable*. Not perfect, but dependable. Not always sharp, but always centered.

This is how you trade with **character**, not just competence.

Final Wrap-Up

By now, you've seen that becoming a consistent, elite-level trader isn't about discovering more strategies—it's about building an **internal architecture** that supports professional behavior every single day.

The Contract Code is your bridge from theory to reality. From "I know what to do" to "I *do* it—on repeat."

You don't need to trade better tomorrow.
You need to honor your system *today*—and do it again, and again, and again, until it becomes who you are.

Commitment → Ritual → Identity.

That's the real code.
That's what makes you untouchable.

10 Advanced Tactics to Reinforce Trading Discipline

These tactics come from books, tutorials, videos, and the occasional private group. I've collected what works—not what's trendy—to give you tools you can apply right now, before you're funded. Some are overlooked. A few are even a little gray hat.

1. AI Accountability Partner

Utilize AI avatar platforms like Synthesia to create a digital version of your ideal trading mentor. Record your trading rules and have the avatar deliver them to you daily, reinforcing your commitment through a personalized, interactive experience.

2. The Proteus Effect

Leverage the psychological phenomenon where adopting a specific avatar or persona can influence behavior. By embodying a disciplined trader avatar, you may naturally align your actions with that identity.

3. Public Commitment via Social Media

Make your trading commitments public by posting your daily or weekly goals and results on social media platforms. This public accountability can increase your commitment to your trading plan.

4. Delayed Gratification Jar

Implement a system where you place a small amount of money into a jar every time you adhere to your trading rules. After a set period, use the accumulated funds for a reward, reinforcing positive behavior.

5. Two-Trade Maximum Rule

Limit yourself to a maximum of two trades per day to prevent overtrading and encourage selectivity. This constraint can help maintain discipline and focus on high-quality setups.

6. Emotional State Logging

Before each trading session, document your emotional state and any external factors that might influence your decision-making. Reviewing these records can help identify patterns and improve emotional regulation.

7. Visualization of Negative Outcomes

Regularly visualize the consequences of undisciplined trading, such as significant losses or missed opportunities. This practice can reinforce the importance of sticking to your trading plan.

8. Pre-Trade Checklist Automation

Create an automated checklist that must be completed before placing any trade. This ensures that all criteria are met and reduces impulsive decisions.

9. Weekly Performance Review with a Peer

Partner with another trader to conduct weekly reviews of each other's performance, focusing on adherence to trading plans and emotional control. This mutual accountability can drive improvement.

10. Mindfulness and Meditation Practices

Incorporate mindfulness techniques and meditation into your daily routine to enhance focus, reduce stress, and improve decision-making under pressure.

By integrating these tactics into your trading routine, you can strengthen your discipline and align your actions with your trading identity. Remember, consistency and self-awareness are key to long-term success.

In the next chapter, we'll take all of these systems even deeper—connecting the dots between your mindset, your habits, and your ability to perform under pressure in real time. We'll explore how **mental edge compounds** and how to sustain peak execution *long after the initial motivation fades.*

Get ready for Chapter 10. Because once you're committed, it's time to get fast, fluid, and *fundable.*

CHAPTER 10

Your Funded Future Starts Today

Become the trader your future depends on—starting now.

There's a dangerous lie most traders believe: *"Once I pass the challenge, I'll start trading like a professional."*

Wrong.

If you can't trade like a funded trader now—with small size, with pressure, with discipline—you won't magically transform once someone gives you capital. Funding doesn't change your habits. It magnifies them.

This chapter is your wake-up call. Your funded future doesn't start after you pass a challenge—it starts **now**, in how you think, how you prepare, how you recover from losses, and how you show up when no one's watching.

We're going to build the mindset, systems, and challenge plan to help you **become the funded version of yourself today**—so that when capital arrives, you're ready for it. Not just technically, but emotionally and behaviorally.

Section 1: Flip the Timeline

Funded Behavior First, Funding Later

Most traders operate with a backward mindset. They think: *"Once I pass the challenge, then I'll start acting like a pro."*
But funding isn't a reward for being lucky—it's a mirror for who you already are.

Passing a prop firm challenge doesn't mean you're ready to manage capital. It means you've temporarily hit a benchmark. What separates the traders who keep the account from the ones who blow it within a month is simple: **funded behavior came first.**

This is the mindset shift that changes everything:
You don't *earn* funding and then behave like a pro.
You *behave* like a pro—and that's why you earn and keep the funding.

When you flip the timeline, you stop asking, *"How do I pass?"* and start asking, *"How would a professional behave today?"*

Imagine a Trader Who Trades Like You

Let's make this personal. Imagine someone walked into your office and said:

> "Hey, I trade just like you. I manage risk the way you do. I prep like you prep. I journal—or don't—like you do. I react to losses like you react. I break rules with the same frequency. I'm your clone."

Now… would you give that trader $100,000 to manage?

If the answer is anything less than *an immediate yes,* then congratulations—you've just met the gap between your **fantasy** and your **readiness**.

This isn't about guilt or shame. It's about clarity. If the person who trades like you doesn't deserve a funded account, you now know exactly what needs to be fixed. Not your strategy. Not your indicators. **Your behavior.**

Stop Practicing Chaos

Every time you sit down and deviate from your rules, skip your journal, or overtrade out of boredom, you're practicing chaos. And what you practice, you *perfect.*

If you constantly rehearse impulsive behavior, that's what becomes automatic. So when the pressure of real capital arrives, you default to what you've trained: inconsistency.

The solution is simple: **start practicing the behavior you want to execute when the stakes are high.**

No more "just this once." No more "I'll tighten things up after I pass." Start executing now with the seriousness, clarity, and focus of someone *already managing six figures.*

Reverse Engineer the End Goal

You want to be a calm, confident, consistent trader. Funded. Respected. In control. Cool under pressure.

Now reverse engineer that version of yourself.

Ask:

- How does that trader show up each morning?
- How do they decide when to trade and when to wait?
- How do they size their positions?
- How do they respond to losses?
- What rituals do they never skip?

Write it out. Describe that person in vivid detail. Then ask: *What's one behavior I can match today?*

You don't need to become that version overnight. But every moment you act like them is a rep. And reps build identity.

But how do you actually reverse-engineer a process that works—without winging it or relying on vague instinct?

That's where my systematic method comes in. I've always believed in building trading systems that are measurable, repeatable, and adaptable. One tool I personally use (and built) is called **FxMagnetic**. It's not a magic bullet—it's a framework that helps you act like a professional by thinking in systems.

Here's the short version of how it works:

- **Discover a strategy** that fits your style: FxMagnetic runs thousands of tests using real indicators and candlestick patterns, showing you the best performers based on win rate, drawdown, and consistency.

- **Decide your execution style**: You can follow signals manually or automate the strategy using Autotrader mode—your choice.

- **Track your metrics in real-time**: Know if your strategy is still performing or starting to drift.
- **Re-optimize when needed**: The market changes. Instead of guessing, you adapt based on live data.

This system has helped many of my students stay grounded through volatility, pass prop firm challenges, and trade with more clarity. But here's the real reason I bring it up:

Because it embodies everything we've talked about—**process over prediction, strategy as behavior, discipline as a system**.

You don't need to use FxMagnetic. But you do need a process that reflects the identity you're trying to build. Something that removes the noise, reveals the data, and lets you focus on executing like a professional.

Remember: the tools don't make the trader. But the right tools can help you become the trader you're training to be.

Align Identity > Strategy > Action

Most traders do this backward: they start with action (new strategy, new setup), then try to build discipline around it, and hope their identity will follow.

But performance that lasts is built the other way around:

1. **Identity:** Who are you becoming?
2. **Strategy:** What plan supports that identity?
3. **Action:** What behaviors reinforce both?

When you lead with identity—*I am a calm, rules-based professional*—your strategy becomes a tool, not a crutch. And your actions stop being reactive and start becoming *deliberate.*

Final Word:

You are not training to become a trader after funding.
You are training to prove that you already are one.

Flip the timeline. Behave like you've already made it—and the results will catch up.

Section 2: Process is the Prize

Let Go of Milestones

Traders love milestones. Getting funded. Doubling an account. Hitting a 10R week. The problem? Milestones are **external rewards** for internal behavior. And when you chase the reward without mastering the behavior, the results fall apart—or worse, create *unsustainable pressure.*

You get funded and feel relief—followed by fear. You hit a winning streak—followed by revenge trades to protect the gains. The milestone becomes the *emotional anchor,* and now every trade feels like it has something to prove.

But here's the truth: milestones are side effects, not goals.

The real goal? **Executing with clarity and control—every single time.**

When you trade for behavior, milestones happen anyway. But when you trade for milestones, you often destroy the behavior that created them.

Trade to Be, Not to Win

Most traders wake up thinking, *"I hope I win today."*
Pros wake up thinking, *"I hope I trade well today."*

That's the difference.

If your focus is on being a consistent trader, you'll naturally make consistent decisions. But if your focus is on *winning,* you'll bend your rules, force trades, and fall apart the moment you're down on the day.

Winning is emotional. Being is structural.

The traders who make it don't chase green days—they chase *aligned days.* Days where their behavior matches their values. Where their process was clean. Where they could look at their trades and say, *"I showed up as the version of me that deserves to get funded."*

That's the only win that matters.

Emotional Feedback Over Financial Outcome

Your PnL doesn't tell the whole story. In fact, it often lies.
You can win money on a terrible trade and lose money on a perfect one. If your self-worth and decision-making are tied to outcomes, your emotions will rise and fall with every candle.

That's a recipe for burnout and inconsistency.

Shift your feedback loop. After every trade, ask:

- Did I follow my system?
- Was my execution clean?
- Did I act from clarity—or from emotion?

- What did I learn about myself in that moment?

Those questions are *data-rich*. They tell you what's actually working—and where the cracks in your mindset still live.

Financial feedback matters. But **emotional feedback builds traders.**

Perfect Execution > Perfect Trades

There's no such thing as a perfect trade. Every setup has risk. Every entry has uncertainty. But perfect **execution**? That's completely within your control.

Perfect execution means:

- Entering exactly where your plan says to enter
- Accepting the stop before the trade begins
- Managing the trade without flinching or forcing
- Logging it, journaling it, and reviewing it—regardless of outcome

This is how you build **predictable behavior** in an unpredictable environment.

Traders who obsess over perfect trades chase ghosts. Traders who obsess over perfect execution *become machines.* Machines with emotional control, built-in standards, and scalable performance.

Success = Repetition Without Distraction

Anyone can follow a plan for a day. What separates the pros from the hopefuls is their ability to repeat behavior without letting emotions or boredom interfere.

That's success:

- Repeating your checklist on Day 1, Day 11, and Day 91
- Doing your pre-trade ritual even when you're not "in the mood"
- Following your stop-loss even after three losses
- Journaling a loss with the same presence as a win

It's not sexy. But it's bulletproof.

Every time you repeat a behavior aligned with your identity, you **compound belief**. You prove to yourself that you are the kind of trader who can stay steady while everyone else is chasing highs and avoiding discomfort.

Final Word:

Let go of the scoreboard.

Start asking a different question: *"How precisely did I show up today?"*

Because when you make process the prize, you stop riding the emotional rollercoaster of results. You stop gambling. You stop hoping.

And you start behaving like the trader your future depends on.

Section 3: Practice Without Pressure

You Don't Build Peak Performance in Chaos

Let's kill the myth right now: pressure doesn't make diamonds—it reveals what you've trained.

You don't rise to the occasion in high-stakes moments. You fall back on your **preparation**.

Elite athletes don't run drills under the lights of game day. They practice in silence, in sweat, in solitude—until their movements become automatic. So that when the lights are on, their mind isn't overwhelmed. It's *ready*.

Trading is no different.

If the only time you're practicing execution is *live, with real capital, under emotional pressure,* you're setting yourself up to fail. That's like stepping into a championship ring with no training camp.

The solution? Train without pressure. Simulate the stress. Run mental drills. Build habits *before* the capital shows up.

Let me share another story that proves how powerful controlled, intentional pressure can be.

Last year—on my birthday again—I found myself at Lake Como in northern Italy. My original plan was a relaxed three-day bike ride around the lake. I wanted to experience the views, the villages, the food—without rushing. But when I arrived at the rental shop, there was a problem: all that was left were high-end sport road bikes. No racks. No way to carry my backpack. And I wasn't about to ride 3 days with a laptop bouncing on my back. I'd already made that mistake the year before around Lake Garda.

So I pivoted. I extended my hotel stay in Como town by a night so I can drop my stuff there. And then I gave myself a new challenge: bike the full loop around Lake Como in one day.

That meant 163 kilometers. Over 1,000 meters of elevation. My longest ride ever in a single day.

I started early, pushing through foggy hills and winding switchbacks. I stopped in small towns to refill my water, snap photos, grab fresh Italian food. The climbs burned. The descents were wild—flying downhill at 40 km/h with the wind in my face. Every hour tested me. Not just physically, but mentally. Especially when I hit the halfway mark and realized I still had over 80 kilometers to go.

But here's the thing: I never doubted I'd finish. Not once.

Because I've trained that belief through years of tough runs, long rides, and mindset reps. That belief didn't come from theory. It came from practice. From previous challenges. From building pressure into my own schedule and proving I could handle it.

That's what this section is about—controlled exposure. Choosing to stretch yourself. Choosing pressure before the market applies it. Because the more often you challenge yourself by choice, the less often you'll panic by default. That's where confidence comes from: reps, not luck.

The High-Stakes Simulation Game

Here's your new training ground: structured simulations.

Each week, block off one or two sessions where your only goal is to trade as if you're managing a **seven-figure fund.**

Rules:

- Every trade must pass your full checklist

- No emotional reaction to wins or losses
- Journal immediately after each execution
- Use a timer between analysis and entry
- Log all behaviors, not just outcomes

The catch? Do it in **demo** or **micro-lot accounts**.

This creates what we call *emotional realism without financial risk*. You're still practicing under rules and rituals—but without the capital-based anxiety that warps judgment.

Over time, these simulations create behavioral muscle memory. You learn to follow your edge regardless of whether money is involved.

Weekly Self-Battles

To level up under low pressure, compete against your past self.

Each week, set one behavioral metric to beat:

- Better pre-trade focus
- Fewer impulse clicks
- Cleaner journaling
- Improved rule adherence

Create a simple challenge:

> "This week, I will complete 5 trades with 100% checklist compliance."

Then track it. Score it. Hold yourself accountable—not to results, but to *behavioral sharpness.*

You don't need competition with others. The *you from last week* is the only opponent that matters. And beating them is what fuels long-term mastery.

Build Stress Tolerance Gradually

Emotional composure isn't built in a day. It's built like physical endurance—by gradually increasing your exposure to discomfort, one layer at a time.

Start with small stressors:

- Take a trade *and walk away from the screen*
- Trade with smaller size than usual and focus only on perfect execution
- Purposefully enter into higher-volatility environments with strict rules to stay detached

This process, known as **stress inoculation**, works because it introduces controlled doses of the pressure that usually breaks you.

You're not avoiding discomfort. You're *training with it,* safely and systematically.

Control the Conditions You Can

When pressure hits, the brain scans for control. If it doesn't find any, it panics. That's when discipline collapses.

So your job is to design an environment where you always have something to fall back on:

- A checklist printed and in view
- A pre-defined rule for what happens after two losses in a row

- A trading ritual that centers you before and after sessions
- A practice of journaling emotional states, not just setups

The more control you *create,* the more calm you can maintain—even in unpredictable conditions.

Pressure doesn't go away. But you can design a system that keeps you from becoming reactive inside of it.

Confidence Through Preparation

Confidence is not built from winning trades. It's built from *knowing you've done the work.*

Every journal entry. Every simulation. Every time you walked away instead of clicking impulsively—that's a deposit into your **confidence bank.**

So when the real capital shows up, or when the market gets wild, you don't freeze. You don't flinch. Because your behavior has already been **battle-tested in silence.**

Final Word:

If you want to perform in pressure, *train without it first.*

Practice isn't something you do until you get lucky. Practice is the proving ground of identity. It's where you create the version of you that doesn't crack under stress.

You're not preparing for the next trade. You're preparing for the *next test of your character.*

And when it comes, you'll be ready—because you've rehearsed your greatness in advance.

Section 4: Stop Waiting. Start Operating.

End the Identity Delay

Most traders are stuck in what we can call the *"identity gap."* They're trying to trade like a pro, but still thinking like an amateur. They're in this weird limbo between who they *are* and who they *want to become.*

The result? Hesitation. Overanalyzing. Inconsistent behavior. And endless waiting for the "right moment" to level up.

But here's the hard truth:

> There is no perfect day to start operating like a professional. You don't earn the right to act like a funded trader—you *decide* to.

The moment you stop waiting for external validation—more capital, more wins, more confidence—is the moment you collapse the identity gap. You stop practicing to be a trader. You start *being one.*

Right now. With the account you already have. With the rituals you've already built.

The Internship-to-Pro Shift

Imagine you're interning at a prop firm. You show up, watch the team, take notes, dabble in a demo. You're learning, but no one's relying on your performance.

Then one day, you're handed a real account. No more notes. No more observation. You're the one clicking. The pressure's real now.

Most traders wait for that handoff. But in reality? **No one is coming to promote you.**

If you want to trade like a professional, you have to *stop thinking like an intern.*

That means:

- No more skipping rituals
- No more "half-journaling" your sessions
- No more overtrading "just to see what happens"
- No more treating your small account like it doesn't matter

You act as if *everything counts*—because it does. Your trading behavior now is writing the script for how you'll act when real funding arrives.

Execute Like a Fund Manager Now

Here's a mental shift that rewires behavior fast:

> "What if this was someone else's money?"

If you were managing $100,000 for a serious investor, how would you trade today?
Would you:

- Skip your checklist?
- Trade based on gut feelings?
- Add to losers?
- Increase size after a loss?

Of course not.

You'd be conservative. Structured. Focused. You'd want to protect the capital—and your reputation. You'd slow down and follow your system to the letter.

So here's the move: **Trade your own capital with that same reverence.**

That's not roleplay. That's identity alignment. And every session you show up with that mindset, you're hardwiring the behavior of a *true professional.*

Choose Mastery Over Motivation

Motivation is a mood. Mastery is a lifestyle.

Waiting to *feel* like showing up is a fast track to inconsistency. The pros don't need to feel good—they need to be good. And they train for it every single day.

When you choose mastery, you:

- Follow your rituals even when you're tired
- Log your losses even when they sting
- Size responsibly even after a win streak
- Skip a day of trading when your mind isn't right

This is the secret nobody talks about:

> Mastery looks boring. But it builds bank accounts.

The goal isn't to chase excitement. It's to get addicted to execution. To become the kind of trader who shows up without fanfare, without drama, and quietly stacks elite performance day after day.

Final Word:

You don't need a bigger account.
You don't need permission.
You don't need another confirmation that you're ready.

You just need to start operating like it.

Stop waiting to become the trader you admire. Step into their mindset today. Trade like your future depends on it—because it does.

Section 5: The 90-Day Reset Plan

Final Mission: The Funded Now Challenge

This is it. The transformation from theory to identity. From knowing what to do, to doing it on repeat.

For the next 90 days, you're not trading to "see how it goes."
You're trading to become the person your future account depends on.

The Funded Now Challenge is not about passing a prop firm exam. It's about building the emotional, behavioral, and ritual infrastructure of a true professional—before the funding arrives. Because once capital shows up, there's no time left to build the foundation. That work starts now.

Think of it like my first multi-day ultra—180 kilometers in 6 days around the Tour du Montblanc. My friend Justin and I ran through mountains, rain, and cold. Each day brought a fresh 1,000+ meters of elevation gain. We'd wake up sore, slip on spikes to tackle snow-covered paths, and grind up icy ridges. Wet feet, soaked clothes, frozen hands—we ran anyway. Not because it was comfortable, but because quitting wasn't an option. That run taught me what consistency under pressure really means.

This challenge isn't about perfect trades. It's about perfect execution of process, psychology, and consistency. You already have the tools—this section will walk you through how to use them in a high-accountability structure that permanently upgrades your identity.

30 Days of Funded-Level Behavior

The first phase of the challenge is simple but powerful: trade for 30 days as if you're already managing six figures. Even if you're using demo. Even if it's micro-size.

Rules:

- Treat every trade like a decision on behalf of a client.
- Never break your risk parameters.
- No trade is taken without checklist confirmation.
- No skipping your daily journal, execution review, or pre-market ritual.
- If no clean setup appears, you do not trade.

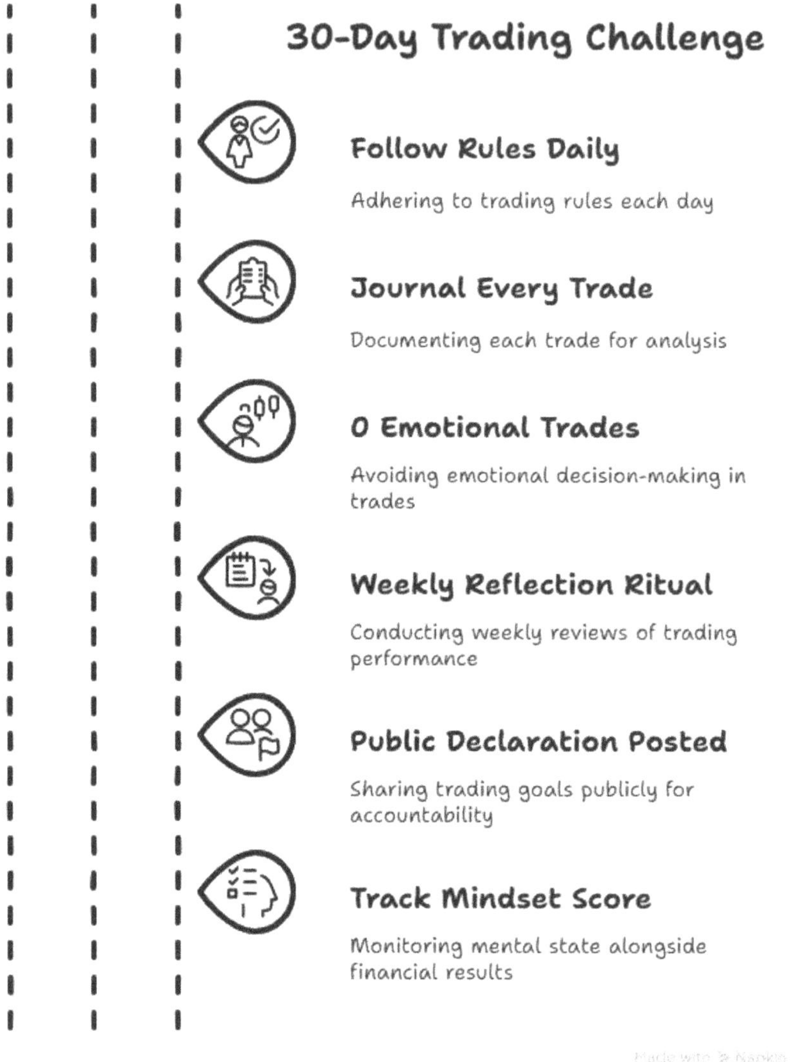

You are becoming **a funded trader in behavior first**—because capital is attracted to consistency, not potential.

Track your daily performance—not your PnL, but your *process alignment.* Rate yourself 1–10 on execution, emotional control, and rule adherence.

Rules, Journals, and Rituals

Every day of the challenge runs on three pillars:

1. Rules:

Your personal trading system is your law. No mid-session edits. No tweaks unless scheduled outside market hours. This builds rule loyalty.

2. Journals:

End every session with three journal entries:

- One win (behavioral or technical)
- One lesson
- One thing to carry into tomorrow

This keeps your mind aligned and evolving. Over time, you'll start to see yourself *growing inside the data.*

3. Rituals:

You must stick to your non-negotiable daily habits:

- Morning mindset primer
- Pre-trade checklist
- Execution scorecard
- End-of-day review
- This is your *operating rhythm.* It's what separates pros from reactionaries.

Measure Mindset, Not Just PnL

You'll want to check your results. That's natural. But your real scorecard isn't your equity curve—it's your **identity curve**.

Each week, reflect on these questions:

- Did I behave like a six-figure trader?
- What emotion tried to hijack me—and how did I respond?
- Where did I stick to structure even when it was hard?

You are learning to **normalize discipline and detach from dopamine.** That is a funded trader's core skill.

Keep a weekly log of mindset wins and psychological patterns. Over time, you'll see that real transformation is not about better entries—it's about *better self-regulation.*

Public Declaration of Intent

You don't have to do this alone.

Make your commitment visible. Share your challenge plan with a trading buddy, coach, or small group. Post it in a journal community. Create light social pressure. This is where motivation becomes *momentum.*

Your declaration could look like:

> "For the next 90 days, I'm trading as if I'm already managing a six-figure account. I will follow my rituals, obey my rules, and review my behavior daily. My goal is not to pass a challenge—but to become the kind of trader who passes *without breaking a sweat.*"

When others know your mission, you rise to meet it. The bar stays high. And your behavior gets sharper—because your identity is now **on record.**

Become the Funded Trader Before You Are

The 90-Day Reset Plan isn't about passing or failing. It's about **becoming.**

By the end of these 90 days, you'll be able to say:

- I've followed my system without exception.
- I've tracked and trained my emotions.
- I've built rituals that carry me through pressure.
- I've acted like the professional I want to be.

And that, right there, is how you get funded—and stay funded.

Final Word:

You don't earn the future by waiting for it.
You earn it by rehearsing it, living it, embodying it *now.*

So take the challenge. Make the commitment. And start trading like someone who's already trusted with capital—because when you do, the capital will come looking for you.

Takeaway Principle:

"You don't get funded and then become a professional. You become a professional—and then you get funded."

This is the core truth traders miss.

Funding is not a finish line. It's not a magic switch. It's not a reward. Funding is an **amplifier**—of who you already are. If you trade with discipline, funding magnifies consistency. If you trade with emotion, funding magnifies chaos.

This is why so many traders pass the challenge but fail the follow-through. They never became the person their account required.
The strategy was ready. But the *identity* wasn't.

So the capital exposed what was untrained:

- The skipped rituals
- The unprocessed losses
- The rule breaks "just this once"
- The belief that the pressure would go away after passing

But the pressure doesn't go away. It increases.
And the only way to meet that pressure is to build the systems, rituals, and mindset of a **funded-level operator—before the money ever shows up.**

That's what this chapter—and this challenge—has given you.

Final Wrap-Up

In Chapter 10, we've flipped the script.

You now understand that your journey isn't about finding the perfect setup, passing a challenge, or getting "lucky" with a funded account. It's about building a **behavioral foundation so solid** that any capital you receive is simply fuel to scale your existing process.

You've learned to:

- Reverse-engineer your identity from the future you want
- Trade for process, not PnL
- Simulate pressure so it doesn't shock your system
- Stop waiting for permission and start operating like a pro
- Lock it all in with a 90-day reset that rewires your default behavior

This is your final internal upgrade before everything changes.

Because from here on out, you're not chasing funding. You're behaving in a way that attracts it.
Not because you're perfect—but because you're **predictable, prepared, and professional.**

And when that's who you are, it's only a matter of time before the market, the firm, or the capital aligns with your performance.

10 Insider Tactics to Think, Trade, and Win Like You're Already Funded

These tactics weren't invented by me—they were collected. I've found them in trading books, deep-dive tutorials, YouTube videos, and the occasional private group or paid course. Some are well-hidden, others are just underused—but together, they form a playbook of practical, powerful ways to upgrade how you trade.

1. "Invisible Capital" Mental Trick

Open a separate trading account with a small balance and mentally treat it as if you're managing a six-figure fund. This psychological shift can help enforce discipline and risk management, as the perceived stakes are higher.

2. AI-Powered Emotional Journaling

Utilize AI tools to analyze your trading journal entries for emotional language patterns. This can help identify subconscious biases and emotional triggers that affect your trading decisions.

3. Simulated High-Stakes Trading

Regularly practice trading sessions in a simulated environment where you impose strict rules and penalties for deviations. This builds muscle memory for disciplined trading behavior without financial risk.

4. Behavioral Scorecard System

Develop a daily scorecard to rate your adherence to trading rules, emotional control, and execution quality. Over time, this quantifies your behavioral improvements and highlights areas needing attention.

5. "No-Trade" Practice Days

Designate specific days where the goal is to follow your trading routine without executing any trades unless all criteria are met. This reinforces patience and discipline, focusing on process over action.

6. Pre-Trade Visualization Ritual

Before each trading session, spend a few minutes visualizing successful execution of your trading plan, including handling potential losses calmly. This mental rehearsal can enhance performance under pressure.

7. Accountability Partner System

Pair up with another trader to review each other's trading plans and journals regularly. This external accountability can reinforce disciplined behavior and provide new perspectives.

8. Delayed Gratification Technique

Implement a rule where profits from trading are only withdrawn or used after a set period, reinforcing long-term thinking and reducing impulsive decisions.

9. Stress Inoculation Training

Gradually expose yourself to higher-stress trading scenarios in a controlled manner to build emotional resilience. This could include increasing position sizes slightly or trading during more volatile periods under strict rules.

10. Public Commitment Declaration

Announce your trading goals and rules publicly, such as on social media or within a trading community. This creates social pressure to adhere to your plan and can enhance commitment.

By integrating these strategies into your routine, you can cultivate the mindset and discipline of a funded trader, positioning yourself for long-term success.

CONCLUSION

The Market is a Mirror. Discipline is Your Weapon. This Book is Your Training Ground.

You've made it to the end. Not just of a book, but of a transformation.

What you hold in your hands isn't just 10 chapters of advice—it's a blueprint. A manual. A mirror. And most importantly, a challenge.

Because here's the hard truth the market doesn't advertise: **It doesn't care what you know. It cares who you are.**

Every time you sit at the charts, the market shows you a reflection—not of the strategy you're using, but of the *identity you're trading from.* That's why this tagline isn't just clever words. It's a distilled reminder of the mission you've chosen to take on:

- **The market is a mirror.**
  It shows you where you're strong—and where you're still cracked. It reflects your hesitation, your overconfidence, your fear, your hope. And it does it without apology. The charts don't lie, and they don't care. They simply expose.

- **Discipline is your weapon.**
  Not indicators. Not setups. Not some secret course.
  Discipline is the sharpest edge you have. It cuts through noise. It holds you together under stress. It keeps you consistent when emotion wants chaos. Every system, ritual, and drill in this book exists to sharpen that weapon. But only *you* can swing it.

- **This book is your training ground.**
  What you've just completed isn't passive. It's active. These chapters weren't designed to inform—they were built to **transform.** Each section was a rep. Each prompt was a drill. Each mindset shift was a psychological upgrade.

You've now trained the following:

- Emotional awareness under pressure
- Identity-driven execution
- Detachment from dopamine
- Resilience after loss
- Consistency without outcome addiction
- Structure over randomness
- Process over perfection
- Internal confidence over external validation

That is not theory. That is *armor.*

But here's the catch—training is never finished.

The elite trader doesn't close this book and say, "Got it."
They say, "Let's go again."

They revisit rituals. They re-do the 90-Day Challenge. They journal with brutal honesty. They treat mastery like a loop, not a ladder.

This is how you shift from chasing to **compounding**.
From dabbling to **dominating**.
From *trading setups* to *trading identity*.

So now, ask yourself:

- When I open my charts tomorrow, who am I becoming?
- Am I reacting—or rehearsing?
- Am I showing up like I trade six figures—or waiting for someone to give me permission?

This journey doesn't end here. It resets here.

The book gave you the blueprint. The drills gave you the muscle. The mirror gave you the truth.

Now the market will give you the test.

Not a test of knowledge.
A test of identity.
A test of discipline.
A test of whether or not you'll finally stop chasing someone else's strategy and start living your own.

So here's your new internal script:

> I am no longer an emotional trader.
> I am a disciplined operator.
> I trade with clarity, structure, and presence.
> I do not fear the market. I study it.

> I do not wait to become the trader I want to be—I behave like them now.
> The market is my mirror. And I am ready to face it.

This is your edge.

This is your moment.

Now close the book—and go earn your future.

Conclusion: The End of the Book – The Beginning of Mastery

You've reached the final page. But this isn't the end. It's the **start of everything real**.

This book didn't promise you a shortcut. It didn't hand you a secret strategy or a magic indicator. Because those things don't create consistent traders—**you do**.

What you've done is far more powerful:
You've confronted yourself.
You've trained your identity.
You've reshaped the way you think, feel, and act in the markets.

You now understand that trading success doesn't come from predicting the next candle—it comes from **predicting yourself**. From becoming someone who can stay composed, stay structured, and stay aligned with a process no matter how wild the chart gets.

That's the real funded mindset. That's what separates those who dabble from those who dominate.

Over these ten chapters, you've built the internal architecture of a professional:

- You learned how the market reflects you back to yourself.
- You broke the illusion of funding and rewired your emotional triggers.
- You trained your mind for discipline, not dopamine.
- You swapped perfectionism for process.
- You learned how to operate under pressure, not react to it.
- And most importantly—you built a system for becoming the trader you've always wanted to be.

This is not the end of your growth. It's the foundation of your evolution.

Keep this book close. Revisit the drills. Reread the mindset shifts. Redo the 90-Day Reset Plan when you feel yourself drifting.
This isn't a one-time transformation—it's a **lifetime practice**.

A Final Word of Hope

You're going to have hard days.
You're going to feel like you've regressed.
You're going to get stopped out, make mistakes, lose focus.

That doesn't mean you've failed.

It means you're a trader. And if you keep showing up with integrity and structure, you'll keep rising—even when the results take time to show up.

You're not here to be perfect. You're here to be consistent.
And consistency—done long enough—is *unbeatable.*

Need Support or Have Questions?

I didn't write this book to lecture. I wrote it to connect—with real traders, like you, who are serious about growth. If you've read this far, it means you're committed to doing the work. And that's the kind of trader I want to hear from.

If you have questions, feedback, or just want to share your journey—I'd love to hear from you.

Email us: support@fxmagnetic.com
Visit us: www.fxmagnetic.com

Whether you're struggling with execution, want help refining your system, or need a community that *actually gets it*—we're here.

Thanks for reading. To your trading success,

Rimantas Petrauskas

Leading Traders to Victory Since 2009

Parting Words

You don't need more information.
You don't need more indicators.
You just need to trust the process—and trust that your new identity can hold under pressure.

You're not the same trader who started this book.
Now it's time to prove it.

The market is waiting.
Show it who you've become.

www.ingramcontent.com/pod-product-compliance
Lightning Source LLC
Chambersburg PA
CBHW050524240926
51846CB00003B/682
9786090808849